CATS

YANN ARTHUS-BERTRAND

This book is dedicated to all the cat-lovers
who so graciously agreed to come to the studio with their cat—
whether they are illustrated in this book or not.
With thanks to Christiane Paillard, Nicole Godier,
and Jacqueline and André Jocquel.

I would like to give special thanks to my two assistants:
Françoise Jacquot, who took care of scheduling,
and Marc Lavaud, for lighting, along with Jean–Philippe Piter,
who was kind enough to offer new ideas.

The film was developed by the GT3P laboratory
in Saint-Rémy-l'Honore.
The photographs were made using a Mamiya RZ 67
and a Canon Eos 1, with Godard flashes.

Thanks, too, to the entire Sotexi staff, particularly Giselle Nicot.
Films: Kodak Ektachrome 100 X
Photographs distributed by Yann Arthus-Bertrand.

CATS

YANN ARTHUS-BERTRAND

TEXTS BY

DANIÈLE LARUELLE

CONSULTANT

SABINE PAQUIN
International feline judge

TRANSLATION BY

SALLY LARUELLE

BARNES
&NOBLE
BOOKS
NEW YORK

ONCE THERE WALKED...THE CAT

This is how the cat in a Rudyard Kipling story addresses the woman who has used her magic powers to enslave some of the wild beasts of the forest—the dog, the horse and the cow. The cat has taken care not to be bewitched: it comes of its own accord to claim its rightful place by the fireside, and charms the woman by playing with the baby and devouring the dreaded mouse. This apparently innocent children's story in fact captures both the real and mythical essence of the cat. The playful little pet with its gentle purr reverts into a dangerous predator as soon as it's let loose, and even if well fed, behaves like a sadistic killer. It is still "the cat who goes through the Wet Wild Woods, waving his wild tail and walking by his wild lone." Some have even suggested that it is the cat who tamed man—unless it actually tamed woman, as in Kipling's story.

Indeed, throughout the ages, from one culture to another, the cat has always been associated with femininity. As Kipling knew, and as the snake in the garden of Eden taught us, it's a short step from woman to devil: the cave woman in his story is a kind witch, and the cat a worthy descendant of Lucifer, the angel of light whose pride led to his fall. Because of these dubious connections, the

"I am not a friend,

and I am not a servant.

I am the Cat

who walks by himself,

and I wish

to come into your Cave."

poor cat has undergone many trials and tribulations in the Western world. *Felis catus* was sanctified, deified and embalmed in the Egypt of the Pharaohs; considered protector of home and childhood in the Gallo-Roman era; then in the Middle Ages condemned to be burned at the stake, ritually sacrificed or simply tortured!

This sad state of affairs persisted in certain places until the early nineteenth century, but could not stop the irresistible ascension of Master Cat: mouse hunter and rat killer extraordinaire, he protected lofts and granaries, and helped keep the plague at bay; his decorative grace soon won him a place in drawing rooms, and the admiration of the powerful, such as French statesman Cardinal de Richelieu, who caused quite a stir by bequeathing part of his fortune to his fourteen cats! The cat padded on velvet paws into the literature of the sixteenth and seventeenth centuries, and was adopted by many Romantic writers for the very "darkness" which had been its downfall in the Middle Ages. It then became a favorite companion to many a poet, settling down among the stacks of books and papers, to watch over their writings much as it used to observe the strange spells of the alchemists.

The brief overview of the adventures of the cat in the Western world demonstrates the ambivalence of human feelings toward an animal which retains a certain mystery—as mankind generally mistrusts what it doesn't understand, we associate this mystery with black magic. The tiger in the London Zoo inspired the poet Paul Valéry to write two pages which come close to defining this elusive feline quality: "I fall into a reverie before this impenetrable animal being (…). In my innocence, I search its admirable muzzle for human qualities. I am held in its grip by its expression of impassive superiority, of power and of absence (…) What completeness, what absolute egotism, what sovereign isolation! Its full potential is ever imminent. This creature leaves me dreaming of a vast empire."

Such reflections could also be applied to the cat, the tiny distant cousin of the Great King of the felines, but the qualities that make the tiger so gloriously imperial are merely misplaced pride and self-importance in the cat. It is too small for such lofty ambitions—at least in the eyes of humans, who, after all, tamed the horse and the dog. In the early Middle Ages, when the Christian church sought to consolidate its conquests, the cat's empire was thought to be that of evil. This naturally Luciferian creature demonstrated its supreme wickedness with its noisy love-life and sensuality. No wonder, then that women were portrayed meeting their lovers at night or going to the devil's Sabbaths—veritable orgies—disguised as cats. When these "witches" were captured, they were burned along with some innocent cat. Other women were burned as heathens too, just because they took care of the handicapped, knew herbal recipes or had mysterious powers. And the cat, who befriended the poor and asked nothing in return, was always burned with them. The church asserted its power with these spectacular acts and made the cat its scapegoat, a symbol of wantonness and obscurantism.

The Age of Enlightenment heralded a brighter chapter in this dark and bloody history. At the court of Louis XV—who loved Persian cats—a certain François Augustin Paradis de Moncrif was the first to sing the praises of the feline race in his *History of Cats,* published in 1727. He was greatly ridiculed for this work, however, as the Age of Reason was still one of ambivalence: some ladies fainted at the sight of a cat, others cultivated their company, wrote verses to them and had tombs erected for them. In *Natural History,* written by French naturalist Georges Buffon some thirty years after Moncrif's text, there is a hateful portrait of the cat, totally lacking in scientific objectivity. Moncrif may have erred in his excessively romantic portrayal and some of his writings now seem ridiculous, but at least he demonstrated, with scholarly quotations, poems and proverbs, that the cat has always been part of society; it has always had enemies, but it has also always had influential supporters.

Historical records concentrate so much on persecution and on witches' trials that we guiltily begin to wonder how poor *Felis catus* survived the carnage at all. But history never mentions the affection of anonymous cat-lovers for a creature which, after all, was both useful ratter and pleasant companion. The true history of the cat has yet to be written, and perhaps will always remain as discreet as a feline's soft footsteps on sand.

The cat is indifferent to its past and cares nothing for its future; it has nine lives, after all, and has thrived despite its woes. It has diversified too, thanks to secret admirers and breeders. By the late nineteenth century, it had become so popular that the first cat shows were organized. Institutions were created to define the standards of the various breeds and to maintain them through selective breeding. The age of the champion cat had dawned—a feline aristocracy, which will be our guide throughout this book. Discover the cat in all its shapes and forms, its relationship to man, to time and place, its role in folklore and the arts, through these portraits of cats and portraits of cat-lovers; birds of a feather, after all! As for all the meanings of the word feline—dip into this book, and you'll see for yourself.

SHORTHAIR

CATS

KORAT

The Korat, from Thailand, is a medium-sized cat with a rounded back, creating an impression of power without heaviness. The tail and legs, ending in oval paws, must be proportionate to the body. The uniform blue-gray coat is fine and glossy, lying close to the body.

The tips of the fur give the coat its silver sheen. The muzzle and pads are a dark blue-gray or lavender color. The head, viewed from the front, is heart-shaped, accentuated by the arched eyebrow ridges. The nose is rounded just above the muzzle, and is neither too long nor too short, with a "stop" at the base of the forehead. The well-developed chin must be neither pinched nor pointed. The large ears are wide at the base, set high on the head and covered in short, tight fur. The round, wide-open eyes are preferably bright green, but may also be amber-colored.

In 1959 an American breeder was given a pair of Korats from Thailand, and she imported other cats to begin a breeding program in the West. Thanks to the pedigree, we can trace the origin of the various lines back to Thailand, where this cat is considered to bring good luck. The Bangkok library has drawings and manuscripts about the Korat dating from 1350 to 1767. We can assume, therefore, that the breed has survived practically pure, even if the ancient descriptions seem fanciful and somewhat Asian in phrasing: "The fur of its coat has roots the color of clouds, tips the color of silver, and its eyes shine like dewdrops on a lotus leaf."

_____

Ejalma d'Osiria de Passaya of Yun Agor, Fyindee de Yun Agor d'Orfeny and Graval I de Yun Agor d'Orfeny (ABOVE), Korats, belonging to Mrs. Claudine Dotte.

RUSSIAN BLUE

The Russian Blue has a graceful, elongated body with slender legs and small oval paws. It is medium-sized, with an elegant neck and a long, tapering tail. Its double coat, with a silver sheen, distinguishes it from other Blues. Its fur is short, thick, very fine, and stands out slightly from the body, unlike the Korat's close-lying coat. The head is short and wedge-shaped. The nose and forehead are straight but there is a slight curve beginning at the level of the eyebrows. The ears are large and rather pointed, with such fine skin that they look transparent; they are scantily covered with fur inside.

This cat with its beautiful bright green gaze also differs from the Korat in that its eyes are almond-shaped. Round eyes are not acceptable in a Russian Blue, and neither is a massive or Siamese-type body. Otherwise known as "Archangel Blue," "Spanish Blue" or "Maltese," the Russian Blue was introduced into England in the mid-1800s by sailors returning from Russia, and, like many other cats, keeps its origins a close secret, but is thought to come from the northern regions. During World War II, the breed nearly died out; in order to save it, breeders crossed it with British Blue and Siamese,

which was disastrous. Apart from the morphological changes, the resulting cats did not have the characteristic double coat. During the 1960s concerted efforts were made to return to the original type and keep it. On a more worldly note, the breed boasts a famous aristocrat: the very noble Vashka, who was the companion of Nicholas I, czar of Russia from 1825 to 1855.

Sascha de Nydow and Saskia de Nydow, Russian Blues, belonging to Mr. and Mrs. Bernhard Mühlheim.

BRITISH SHORTHAIR

"**W**e would do well to look to the gutters for our education," wrote Moncrif in his History of Cats in 1727. The nineteenth-century cat-lover and painter Harrison Weir must have agreed with him, as he hand-picked cats from the gutters of Great Britain to breed and show, thereby raising the common or garden alley cat to the rank of "British Shorthair." This terribly colonialist appellation was used at the time to refer to a variety of continental household cats, and was the cause of much confusion, until specific breeding programs defined the precise standards for British and European Shorthairs, according to morphological differences.

Nowadays, the British Shorthair still has a slightly rugged look which betrays its common origins. It is a medium-sized cat, with a sturdy, muscular body, broad shoulders, short robust legs, and a deep, rounded chest. The tail is thick at the base, and should be as long as two-thirds of the body. The head must not be too short, and is round, like the muzzle. The eyes are also round, and are orange, gold or copper-colored; in the case of silver-coated cats, the eyes should be green, and white cats can be odd-eyed.

The eyes are set quite wide apart, accentuating the width of the nose, and there is a very slight stop between the nose and the well-defined forehead. The very thick, short hair covering the forehead gives it a rounded look. The ears are quite wide at the base, and quite small, with rounded tips. Its short, plush fur makes this cat look round and fluffy—most inviting to the touch! With its sweetly innocent, picture-book face, it looks just like a cuddly toy come to life.

Vincent van Lady's Home, Whoopy van Lady's Home, and Grisella van Kievietsdel, British Blue Shorthairs, belonging to Els H. Franssen van der Meer.

CATS ON SHOW

As early as 1598, the English showed cats at a fair; three centuries later, they were also the first to hold cat shows as we know them today. The first of these took place at the Crystal Palace in London, in 1871. It was organized by Harrison Weir, a famous artist and cat-lover, who also defined the first standards. The event was so successful that it spread to other English towns, then to the Continent: the first Paris cat show was held in 1896 at the Jardin d'Acclimatation.

The English kept their lead, however, as they had already founded the world's first feline society, the National Cat Club, in 1887. France and Belgium founded their own Cat Clubs in 1913, and associations of this kind began to flourish both in Europe and America. The pedigree show-cat was born, and with it, the science of feline breeding, to which we owe the shapes and colors of today's competition cats.

Avram Van Diaspora,
Lilac British Shorthair,
belonging to Mrs. Béatrice Passin.

THE PHILOSOPHICAL CAT

The cat has long been a source of inspiration to the thinker. Its mysterious, compelling presence has made it the ideal companion for the solitary philosopher, the privileged guest in the alchemist's secret study or the hermit's cell, and the muse on the poet's writing-desk.

The poet Théophile Gautier described the cat as a philosophical creature, and writer Pierre Loti called it contemplative and enigmatic. The latter was inspired to describe it in metaphysical terms:

"In our absolute ignorance, our inability to know anything, what surprise—and perhaps terror—we would feel if we could penetrate through the strange windows of those eyes into the mystery of the little brain beyond. Are these familiar creatures so very inferior to us, so very far from us... or are they terribly close? Is the veil of shadows that masks the meaning of life much thicker over their eyes than over our own? But no, none of us will ever, ever be able to de-

cipher anything at all of the minds of these voluptuous little creatures, which so love to be held, caressed, almost kneaded in our hands..."

Maybe the aura of mystery we attribute to the cat is just the projection of human doubts about destiny; perhaps the interrogation we read into its sphinx-like stare is just the reflection of our own anxiety. We can philosophize all we like, but sooner or later we reach out and touch the irresistible little creature, whose

role is perhaps simply to remind us of life's sweetness, by reacting with such pleasure to our touch.

ABOVE: *Gimini Silver du Rio d'Erclin, Silver Classic Tabby British Shorthair, belonging to Mr. and Mrs. Georges Vallez.*

RIGHT: *Aldo de la Chezine, Cream British Shorthair, belonging to Mr. and Mrs. André Martaud.*

SELKIRK REX

Hello, I'm the Selkirk Rex. My nickname is the "Sheepcat," though I'm called after a breed of rabbit (and sometimes I hop, too)! My curly coat is a rarity that I share with the little long-eared herbivore, and with my cousins from Devon and Cornwall, but otherwise we look quite different.

My English cousins and I also have our humble origins in common: we were discovered in litters of ordinary kittens, after a natural mutation. The breeders thought we were so pretty that they decided to establish our breed. I am the youngest Rex to date; my ancestor, Miss Pesto, was born in Wyoming in 1987, of a common American mother and unknown father. She was adopted by Mrs. Newman, a Montana breeder of Persian cats, and moved up into high society! Her first partner, a black Persian called Photo Finish, gave her three curly kittens, so the Selkirk is genetically dominant, because just one Selkirk parent was enough to produce these curly little cats. I'm very proud of my ancestors—I owe them my robust, gracefully rounded body—but I'm even prouder of my three kinds of curly hair, and of my eyebrows and whiskers!

PRECEDING DOUBLE PAGE:
Halvane du Parc

ABOVE AND RIGHT:
White Selkirk Rex,
and Happy-Jolly du Park,
Solid Red Selkirk Rex, belonging
to Mr. and Mrs. Jacques Courdille.

A LITTLE DEVIL

Artists everywhere have long been fascinated by the cat's meticulous personal hygiene program! It featured in the medieval *Books of Hours,* and on the famous Japanese prints.

For the cover of Champfleury's book, *Cats,* Manet chose to immortalize the cat as an indecent little creature, seen from behind with its tail in the air. In the long-gone days when it was associated with witchcraft, the cat in this curious posture had a particularly sinister reputation: the devil was represented coming to Sabbaths in the form of a gigantic black cat, which

showed itself in this provocative pose to the assembled witches, who then bestowed a ritual kiss on its proffered backside!

We can only wonder at such wild flights of fancy when we see this adorable little Rex, which seems incapable of such devilishness! Its funny little face looks more frightened than frightening; and indeed it is angelically sweet-natured, and quite blameless in its behavior!

Jewel Tiffany Van Zechique,
Red Shaded Cameo Devon Rex,
belonging to Mrs. Marijke Wijers.

DEVON REX

The Devon Rex is a slender cat with a firm, muscular body, long, slim legs and a tapering, pointed tail. Its long, elegant neck carries a wedge-shaped head with high cheekbones, a strong chin, a short, pinched muzzle and a short nose. Its forehead curves back to a flat skull. Its wide-based ears are huge and low-set, giving the cat its impish air. Its large, oval eyes are set on a slight slant. Finally, like all the Rex cats, the Devon Rex has a curly coat.

The first Rex of this kind was discovered in 1960 living in a abandoned tin mine in Devon. It mated with a tortie-and-white female stray, and one of the resulting male kittens had its father's curly coat. This kitten was named "Kirlee" by its adoptive owner, who was aware of the existence of the Cornish Rex: mating was attempted, but the resulting litters were hopelessly straight-haired, and an inbreeding program was therefore used to establish the breed.

ABOVE: Honey Bee Van Zechique, White Devon Rex.
RIGHT: Honesty Van Zechique, Tortie Tabby Devon Rex, belonging to Mrs. Marijke Wijers.

CORNISH REX

The Cornish Rex was the first of all Rex cats, appearing on July 21, 1950. It was a curly little mutant in a litter of ordinary kittens whose mother, Serena, was an unexceptional farm cat. Serena's owner, a breeder of curly-coated Rex rabbits, was charmed by this strange kitten. She was advised to mate it back to its mother, to try to obtain other curly offspring. Two years later, Serena produced an ordinary female kitten and two curly-coated males. This new breed took a while to establish, because one of the kittens disappeared, and the other one was rendered sterile when it was adult. Fortunately, it already had descendants, and the mutant gene was preserved by crossing with Burmese and British Shorthair, which resulted in a diversification of colors, and helped establish a type and avoid inbreeding.

The new cat was called "Cornish" because it was born in Cornwall, and "Rex"... because of the rabbit. The Cornish Rex has a short, dense, curly or wavy coat. Unlike the Devon Rex, it has no guard hairs at all. It has long, crinkled whiskers and eyebrows. It is slimmer than the Devon Rex, with a medium-sized, very muscular body. With its long, slender legs and long, tapering tail, it has all the elegance of a feline greyhound, a characteristic which American breeders have accentuated by crossing it with Siamese and Orientals.

Seen in profile, the head is flat at the top, then curves gently at the forehead, and continues in a straight line to the tip of the nose. The eyes are oval, wide-open and slightly slanting. They may be any color, but must be in keeping with the coat. The large ears are wide at the base and slightly rounded at the tips, but, unlike those of the Devon Rex, they are set high on the head and are more conical in shape. They are covered in very fine hair, but do not have the tufts which adorn the tips of the Devon's ears.

ABOVE: Héloïse de Cléomont, smoky black and white Cornish Rex belonging to Mr. Jean-Pierre Filippi.

LEFT: Carlozio's Raphael Gold, Devon Rex chocolate Tonkinese, belonging to Mrs. Anna Maris Quitela.

OF CATS AND MEN

Why on earth are we so fond of a creature as capricious as the cat? It has nothing to offer us except its furry presence, and it has been a long time since it did us any favors in return for our affection...

In the words of Italian painter Léonor Fini: "Rebels and revolutionaries, oddballs and loners, the lonely, the locked away and the uninhibited all love cats." Perhaps we admire them for the beautifully independent spirit which keeps them from all submission; when a cat disobeys, it's not through any lack of discipline (it obeys when it wants to)—but rather to mark out a sort of mental territory, which teaches us the limits of our influence.

Or perhaps we envy them the perfection of their grace and elegance, their ability to luxuriate in laziness and to live for the present moment, their unabashed narcissism... qualities which may not be crimes, but which are difficult to exploit in human society! In short, "the cat is a warm, furry, whiskered and purring reminder of a lost paradise"—according to Fini again, who paints the cat's detractors in very somber colors: "They defend a certain kind of order, their proprietary instinct is easily threatened, they are weakened by an excessive attachment to objects ("my drapes, my armchair, my steak!"). The arrogant, the envious, the stuffy, the touchy and the thrifty do not like cats. The abject accuse them of their own wickedness, or want to punish them for their beauty."

ABOVE: Gaston,
Framboise du Pen Cuckoo
and Hela d'Aba, Cornish Rex,
belonging to
Mr. and Mrs. Laurent Maillet.

EUROPEAN SHORTHAIR

And here it is, the cat that is loved just for itself, the gentle household pet, the everyday cat, the town cat and the country cat, the ordinary cat in all its glory: the European. Although it arrived in Gaul with the Roman armies, it was not recognized as a distinct breed in cat shows until 1983! Yet it has made a significant contribution to folklore and literature, has been of great service and has paid a high price, especially to skin-merchants and witch-burners.

How could European cat-lovers ignore it, when it stands on every street corner, scoffing at the breeds of greater renown with their more exotic origins? Its very ordinariness has become its distinguishing feature: the European is an average cat, ideally resembling the common household cat, and its main quality is that it lacks the qualities of the other breeds! The European must not have an elongated body like a Siamese or Oriental, nor a "chunky" body like the British or the Exotic Shorthair. It can be from medium-sized to large, and is sturdy, supple and muscular with thick, strong legs proportionate to its body, and a broad, deep chest. Its head is quite big and rounded, but otherwise there is nothing "round" in this cat's appearance.

Its nose is straight, and of the same width all down its length. The base of its forehead is well-defined, but the European does not have a stop—unlike its British cousin, which also has smaller ears. Its round eyes are set well apart at a slight slant, and they can be green, yellow or orange. White cats can have blue eyes, or eyes of different colors. Its fur is short, thick and glossy, with neither the smooth sheen of an Oriental nor the downiness of an American. In short, the European is extraordinarily average!

Glaçon, White European,
belonging to Mrs. Monique Barbotte.

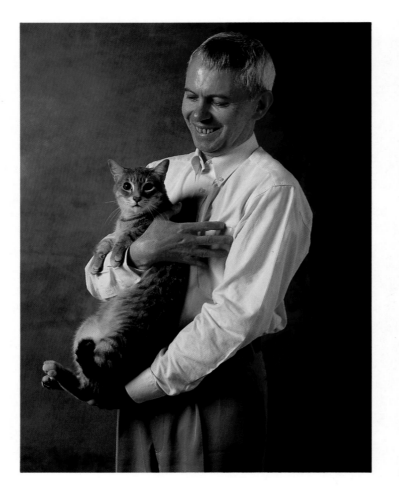

THE ORIGIN OF THE SPECIES

In the eighteenth century, the French naturalist Buffon wrote: "The wild cat mates with the domestic cat, so together they make up one and the same species."

In 1746, Linnaeus, the Swedish naturalist, suggested that our *Felis catus* might be of exotic origin—but he had not studied the European wild cat, which was unknown in Scandinavia. The tricky question of the cat's origins had already caused much ink to flow: as early as the fourteenth century, Gaston Phébus expressed his disagreement with the earlier ideas of Albertus Magnus, and underlined the morphological differences between the wild and the household cat. In 1827, the Dutch naturalist Conrad Jacob Temminck oriented research towards Egypt, homeland of the "Gloved Cat" (*Felis libyca*). The recent study of mummified cats has proved that his intuition was correct. Moreover, we know today that it is very difficult to cross a household cat with a wild one—and when it does happen, the kittens either do not survive, or remain sterile. What's more, unlike the Egyptian gloved cat, our wild cat cannot be tamed, and does not reproduce successfully in captivity.

Danube, Blue Spotted European, belonging to Mrs. Daniela Goll.

PUSSYCAT, PUSSYCAT, WHERE HAVE YOU BEEN?

The domestic cat originated in Egypt, where it was a sacred animal: when a pet cat died, the whole family shaved off their eyebrows in mourning, and anyone known to have killed a cat faced the death penalty. Traces of *Felis domesticus* have been found in ancient times in Crete, Greece and Sicily. Phoenician merchants no doubt made the cat a contraband commodity. The Romans adopted it, and at the end of the fifth century it thrived all over their Empire. Archaeological excavations have revealed its presence in Gaul and Great Britain even before the Roman conquest.

In India, it was mentioned in the Manu laws of 1200 B.C. and was found in sixth century Japan! The last part of the world that our traveling cat reached was America, where it arrived in the eighteenth century, to confront the black rats of the New World.

ABOVE: Zazie, Black and White European, belonging to Mr. Claude Paul Godenir and Mr. Marcel Godenir.

RIGHT: Fugue du Val aux Biches, Brown Classic Tabby European, belonging to Mrs. Jacqueline Monnet.

A CATALOG OF NAMES

Human imagination and inventiveness tend to run riot when choosing a name for the family's favorite feline. In *Old Possum's Book of Practical Cats,* T.S. Eliot dealt with the tricky problem of naming the creature. He tells us that the cat should have three names. The first is an ordinary one for everyday use, the second is:

" ... a name that's particular,
A name that's peculiar, and more dignified,
Else how can he keep up his tail perpendicular,
Or spread out his whiskers, or cherish his pride?."
The third, secret name the cat alone knows and will never tell:
"His ineffable effable Effanineffable
Deep and inscrutable singular Name."

Elodie des Mézières,
Golden Classic Tabby European,
and her kittens,
belonging to Ms. Suzanne Piqué.

THE SPHYNX

No, I'm not a four-legged bat, or a medieval gargoyle come to life... Don't you like me? Do you find my nakedness indecent? Come, come, am I any more naked than you? You want to know where I come from? Well I shan't tell you... because I am a sphinx, after all, so I ask the questions! And I only answer when it suits me, because I'm also a contrary cat.

Wouldn't you like to stroke my soft skin? It would be a change from fur! But maybe you don't like my wrinkles, or the way my muscles show through my skin—or maybe you think I'm ungainly...?

I'm actually a kind of Devon Rex, minus the fur... which makes me all the more of a mutant. In any case, those Rex cats are just beginners at the mutation game, but I'm an old-timer! I have ancestors on pre-Colombian engravings; scientists spotted me in 1830 in Paraguay and in 1900 in Mexico—and now that I'm being seriously bred, you'll just have to put up with me!

Phalaenopsis Georgette à Poil!,
Brown Tortie Tabby and
White Sphynx, belonging to
Mr. Patrick Challain and
Mr. Guy André Pantigny.

JAPANESE BOBTAIL

The Japanese Bobtail is svelte and muscular, with a rounded muzzle and a triangular head; it owes its name to its short pom-pom tail. Its high cheekbones and slanting eyes seem to confirm its Asian origins, which go back to the seventh century. When standing, its longer hind legs are bent; when sitting, it often raises one of its forepaws, a gesture which is immortalized in many Japanese statuettes called

"Maneki-neko" (Beckoning Cats). They are supposed to bring wealth when their left paw is raised, happiness when it's the right one... and when the living animal is tri-colored, it keeps evil spirits at bay!

ABOVE: *Passetis Chase.*
LEFT: *Izumo von der Baderstadt.*
RIGHT: *Ioko-Omo von der Baderstadt. Japanese Bobtails, belonging to Mr. Rolf Voehringer.*

MADE IN THE U.S.A.

The cat on the previous page is an American Shorthair, an immigrant that headed West with the pioneers. Its body shape is very similar to that of its European cousins, but it has a rougher coat—a reminder of its adventurous life no doubt—and of course it's bigger, like all things American! As for us, we are the curly-eared "American Curl"—we appeared after a chance mutation in the early 1980s.

As we're so new, our type is not quite fixed yet, apart from our ears, which are wide at the base and curl up, ideally in smooth arcs. Our fur can be short, dense and close-lying, or semi-long, smooth and silky, without an undercoat or ruff. What else? Well, we're medium-sized, with a more or less elongated body. Our head is longer than it is wide; we have a straight nose, without a stop, and a gently curving forehead. Our large, oval eyes are set well apart, and they correspond with our coat, which can be any color.

───────────

PRECEDING DOUBLE PAGE:
*Miribu's Bustopher Jones
of Phalaenopsis,
Brown Classic Tabby American
Shorthair, belonging to
Mr. Guy André Pantigny.*

ABOVE: *Hollywood Chewing Gum
de Cour Saint-Eloi,
Red and White American Curl,
belonging to Ms. Florence Prescott.*

RIGHT: *Harmonie d'un soir
des Fleurs du Mal,
American Curl, belonging to
Mr. Christian Doublet.*

BURMESE

The elegant figure of the Burmese distinguishes it both from the slimmer Oriental and the heavier European. It has a medium-sized, vigorous, muscular body, with a strong, rounded chest and a perfectly straight back. Its legs are relatively slender and well-proportioned, with small round paws. Its head is rounded, tapering to a short triangle. It has full cheeks (especially the male). The medium-sized ears are broad at the base, set well apart and tilting slightly forward. There is a break between nose and forehead. The muzzle must not be pinched, and is characterized by a strong lower jaw and well-developed chin. The lower line of the eyes should be rounded, but the upper line slants towards the nose. Eye colors may vary from yellow to amber, with a preference for gold. The fur is short, fine, very glossy and satin-like, with practically no undercoat. The coat should have no marks or stripes, but certain coat colors gradually lighten toward the sides and belly.

The Burmese have their origins in a cat called "Wong Mau," brought back from Rangoon to the U.S.A. in 1930. At first it was crossed with a seal point Siamese called "Tai Mau," and produced some Siamese-type kittens and others that looked like their mother. By mating the non-Siamese kittens with each other and with their mother, the Burmese breed was fixed, and was officially recognized in America in 1936.

Registration had to be suspended in the 1940s, however, as the importance of the Siamese line was threatening to eliminate the characteristics of the original breed. The American breeders got back to work on the selection process; meanwhile, the English, who had imported Burmese in 1947, were developing their own breeding program, and recognized the breed officially in 1952. The following year, the American Burmese was registered again, this time for good. Today, the American type can be distinguished from the British by its more robust, less oriental morphology.

ABOVE: Kittens of Eesara cha Iro No Ran, Sable Burmese, belonging to Mrs. Béatrice Wood.

RIGHT: Houdette de Treuzy known as Eliza, Chocolate Burmese, belonging to Mr. Sébastien Bonutti.

TONKINESE

The Tonkinese has only the most distant connection with the Orient, because the breed was in fact developed in America as a result of crossing Burmese and Siamese.

It was recognized in Canada in 1974, and in the United States in the 1980s, but has yet to be officially registered in Europe—although it is recognized by independent clubs.

In appearance, it is the perfect synthesis of its parents—it's more svelte that the Burmese, but heavier than the elongated Siamese. Its body color is like that of the Burmese, but it has the dark Siamese points. Its head is not as round as that of the Burmese, nor as triangular as that of present-day Siamese. It has its own special charm, with its aquamarine or pale turquoise eyes.

This genetic hybrid should please those who are nostalgic for past esthetic standards, like those of the first English Burmese and the early, more rounded Siamese.

ABOVE: Hug Cha Iro No Ran, known as Duchesse, Natural Mink Tonkinese, belonging to Mrs. Jocelyne Majus.

BURMILLA

Like the Tonkinese, the Burmilla is part Burmese, but it was not developed as a result of breeders' efforts. In fact it was the accidental fruit of an "unscheduled" love affair!—between a female lilac Burmese and a male Chinchilla Persian, both belonging to Baroness Miranda von Kirchberg. As the owners of "quality" cats attach great importance to the purity of the breed, one can imagine that the lady in question was hardly overjoyed to learn of this illegitimate affair! But when the fraudulent kittens were born in Great Britain in 1981, they were so irresistibly cute that they made up for their parents' wicked ways, and became the founders of an authentic new breed. The Burmilla resembles the Burmese in its elegant shape, slender legs, slanting eyes and the general appearance of its head. It has the Chinchilla's dark penciling on its cheeks and around its eyes—which are always a beautiful green—and the characteristic tipping which gives the coat its highlights. Its fur is thick and close-lying, longer than that of the Burmese. The colored tips of its hairs can be all the Burmese colors (sable, chocolate, blue, lilac, red, cream) or black like the Chinchilla on a golden or silver undercoat.

PRECEDING PAGE, ABOVE AND RIGHT: Thamakan Silver Jeannet, Silver Burmilla, belonging to Mrs. Anna Maria Quintela, photographed with Mrs. Marianne Paquin.

CATS AT PLAY

In his *History of Cats*, Moncrif describes their "natural gaiety," the playful nature that we find so appealing. He even accords them a certain wit and intelligence: "… in the cat, we have an amusing friend, which is fond of us only because it chooses to be so. Every moment it spends with us is a voluntary sacrifice of its liberty, of that versatility which restricts neither its abode nor its pleasures. Indeed, we must consider cats as possessed of still finer qualities. If we care to analyze their feelings, so to speak, what nobility we find! Nothing surprises them, nothing impresses them, all moving things become objects of amusement. They believe that nature is concerned only with their entertainment; they cannot conceive of any other reason for the movement; and when we tease them and make them frolic, do not our antics look to them like so much buffoonery? Thus each side fools the other: and we entertain when we think we are being entertained."

But perhaps we should add, only when puss is in the mood!

THE BOMBAY—A GENTLE PANTHER

The Bombay is a relatively recent breed, resulting from a cross between sable Burmese and black American Shorthair. Its glossy fur is short, close-lying, and must be jet-black to the roots, like its skin, nose and pads. Its round eyes are set far apart, and range in color from gold to copper—no other colors are allowed. The head and muzzle are rounded, it has full cheeks, and medium-sized, broad-based ears which tilt slightly forwards, like those of the Burmese. Its nose is fairly short, with a slight stop between the eyes.

This breed was recognized in America in 1976 and is now fixed, but crossings are still allowed between Bombay and Burmese. It's a mini-panther, which owes its exotic name to its dangerous, Indian cousin... but our little one is gentle and affectionate, as if to contradict the many, age-old legends about the black cat and its wickedness.

Fejuko's Jeanette Isabella, Bombay, belonging to Mr. Michel Le Hir.

EGYPTIAN MAU

In Egypt, homeland of this breed with its finely spotted coat and distinctive gooseberry-colored eyes, "Mau" means "cat." It is reminiscent of the Abyssinian with its strong, supple body, which must be neither heavy nor elongated.

It has a slightly rounded, wedge-shaped head, a short nose, and medium to large ears with furnishings inside. Its forehead is marked with an "M," and its almond-shaped eyes are elongated with fine lines, as if they were made-up. Its tail is marked with rings, and its neck with an open collar. Its hind legs have stripes, most of which do not form complete rings. Its fur is fine, silky and close-lying, with two bands of ticking. The first authentic Maus were introduced into Italy in the 1950s; they then accompanied their owner to the United States where the breed was recognized in 1978.

Meanwhile, British breeders, unable to import the cat because of quarantine regulations, tried to recreate it by crossing Abyssinians with various tabbies and Siamese. The result, which was disappointing in comparison with the original, became known as the Oriental Spotted Tabby.

BEHAVIOR

The paw that this cat has placed so firmly on its "mistress's" hand is a sign of affection and trust... with something dominating about it. Nobody really knows who is master. Specialists can prove that the tame household pet behaves just like its wild brothers when it's outside the home, and becomes kitten-like again when in our company, turning "its humans" into adoptive mothers.

Junglebook Aspen Mist,
Silver Egyptian Mau,
belonging to
Mrs. Ingrid B. Baur-Schweizer.

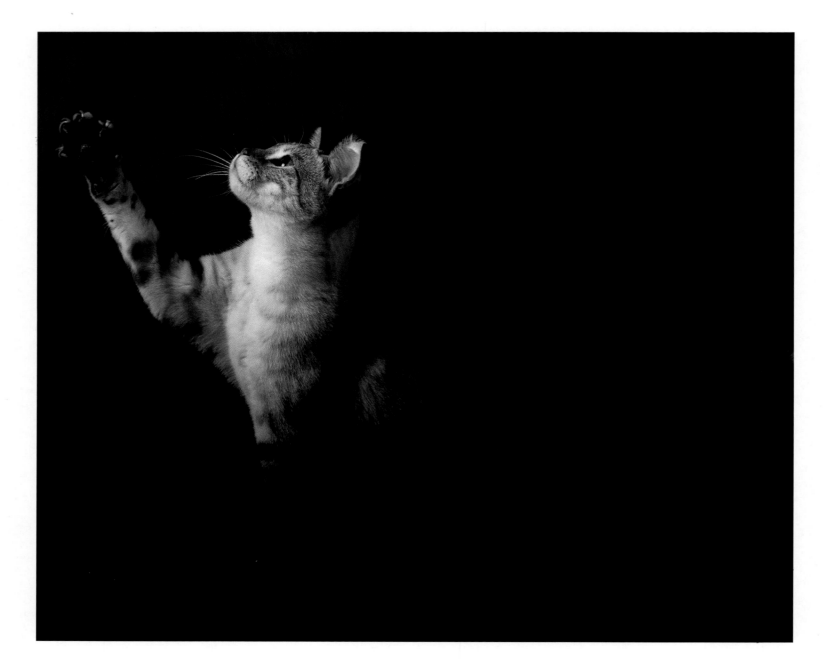

BENGAL

The Bengal is a relatively recent breed, another product of civilized man's efforts to realize his dreams through the science of feline breeding. Man seems to be haunted by the fantasy of having a more or less tame, small-scale model of the terrible wild cats of the jungle in his living-room.

The Bengal is a result of this "Mowgli complex"; an American breeder developed it from a hybrid, produced by mating European or American Shorthairs with Felis bengalensis, an Asian wild cat also known as the "Leopard Cat." The first kittens were mated with Egyptian Maus and other spotted cats. This hybridization program, started in the 1960s, has produced a big, powerful, muscular cat with a strong bone structure, which looks rather like a wild animal. It has a squat neck and a rounded head which seems rather small in proportion to its body. The oval eyes are set well apart, and slightly slanting; the ears point slightly forwards.

The fur is short, thick and rather fluffy-looking, but soft and satiny to the touch. Dark spots cover the back, sides and belly; its head, shoulders and legs are striped, and its tail is ringed, with a dark tip.

At the present time it would seem that this beautiful creature is not always very sweet-tempered, so breeders are trying to mellow its character—which is perhaps a good idea, seeing that the males can weigh up to 17 or 18 pounds!

THE SOCIAL CLIMBER

Like it or not, the cat is a natural climber. I once knew a particularly mischievous puss, who used to love climbing up the burlap-covered walls of its domain, to hang upside down above the doorways and terrorize passing humans with an ear-piercing "miaow" before dropping down to land at their feet!

ABOVE AND FOLLOWING PAGES:
Bengal's hill's Hearty,
Snow Chocolate Spotted Tabby
Bengal, belonging to
Mr. and Mrs. Michel Sfez-Zon.

SINGAPURA

The Singapura and the European Shorthair have their place of origin in common: the street. The Singapura is nicknamed the "Drain Cat" in Singapore, and is very common throughout South-East Asia. It is no doubt thanks to its unloved, underfed ancestors that it is so elegantly small: an adult female weighs no more than two kilos, and a male hardly three!

It was noticed in the mid-1970s by American breeders who took it home in their baggage to turn it into a show breed. So here it is, with its slightly triangular, rounded head, its large ears and its enormous green, yellow or

hazel eyes. Dark lines are pencilled from the brows and outside corner of the eyes, and go down the sides of the nose from the inner corner of the eyes. Its body is svelte and muscular, with strong legs tapering to small, oval feet with dark pink pads. Its ivory and bronze coat is very short, silky and close-lying, with ticking like that of the Abyssinian. There are not yet many of these ex-Asian gutter cats in America... but they are an even greater rarity in Europe.

H-Butterfly du Fort Canning,
Brown Tabby Singapura,
belonging to Mr. Gérard Prescott.

OCICAT

In the mid-1960s, American breeder Virginia Daly was working on a breeding program crossing Abyssinians and Siamese. A Chocolate Point Siamese male and a hybrid female produced an unexpected, completely spotted cat, which was called "Ocicat" (Ocelot + cat). The newcomer became the object of a specific breeding program designed to fix the breed and to have it recognized.

The Ocicat is elegant and powerful, neither too thin nor too heavy, and must look like a small, wild feline. Its head should be neither too triangular nor too round, with full cheeks and a well-developed chin. Its muzzle is quite long, well-defined but not pointed, and its nose has a slight stop. Its large, almond-shaped eyes are very wide apart and slightly slanting; they may be of any color except blue.

Its medium-sized ears are straight, and set well to the sides of the head. It has powerful legs and strong, oval feet. The tail is quite long and slightly tapering. The coat's ticking gives it its clearly-defined "eye-spots." The head is striped, and the tail ringed.

TOP MODEL

To tell you the truth, the secret of my graceful, undulating pose is that, on this particular morning, I didn't feel like showing off my beautifully ocellated belly. So, with all due respect, I was gently and politely forced to do so! Well, as you know, a cat doesn't like to be forced, and in my stubborn little feline head, I began to hatch a plot: escape! So, ever-so-discreetly, ever-so-daintily, I stretched out my elegant leg, just to see… I didn't want to be too hasty—I'm not an alley-cat, after all—and I was enjoying being photographed and fussed over. And have you noticed the way I've draped my tail so beautifully around my dancer's leg? You must admit, I'm the most glamorous creature on the catwalk!

Gitane du Vieux Pont,
Brown Tabby Ocicat,
belonging to Mrs. Suzanne Arelli.

CATS
AND DOGS

Buffon may have been a "naturalist," but he certainly painted a black picture of the cat in order to whitewash the dog, and ever since, the partisans of one or another species have always fought... like cats and dogs! At the heart of this tricky issue lie projections of human feelings, value judgments, and moral attributes ascribed to one or the other animal, so that the cat's friend necessarily becomes the dog's enemy. "Cats have touchy little souls, little souls full of tenderness, pride and capriciousness; they are impenetrable, only revealing themselves to a privileged few... Their intelligence is at least equal to that of the dog, but they never behave with such obsequious submission, such ridiculous self-importance, or such revolting uncouthness. These are elegant, patrician creatures...," wrote Pierre Loti, who also accused the poor old dog of being "irremediably common," and of having "the dirty ways of an upstart." Chateaubriand loved the cat for its "independent, almost ungrateful nature, which means that it attaches itself to no-one, and the indifference with which it moves from salon back to gutter." He also notes that, when we stroke

it, "it arches its back, because it feels physical pleasure, unlike the dog, which feels a stupid satisfaction at loving and being faithful to its master—who rewards it with a kick of his boot."

It is Moncrif who gives us the finest analysis of the differences between our two familiar companions. He explores the reasons for the behavior that makes us take sides so obstinately: "The dog is fond of us because it could not survive without us"; the cat is of a more "fortunate constitution," and therefore "free from all care, never seen to concern itself with tomorrow... Foresight, though we may consider it a worthy quality, is none the less the daughter of fear... A dog may be surrounded by all it needs to satisfy its voracity, but still it does not enjoy the peace of mind which constitutes true happiness; at the very moment of its satisfaction, it is aware of the penury to come; so it mistrustingly hides away a part of its bounty." Perhaps the real debate is whether the fear of going hungry can justify submission?

Hocy du Vieux Pont, Chocolate Silver Spotted Ocicat, belonging to Mr. Fabrice Calmes.

CALIFORNIA SPANGLED

I'm the California Spangled Cat, a pure product of feline breeding techniques! I was first conceived by a Hollywood scriptwriter, Paul Casey, who wanted me to look like the spotted wild cats of Africa. In the 1970s, specialists got to work to create me, mating British and American Shorthairs with a Cairo street cat, a housecat from Malaysia, and a few Siamese thrown in for good measure. Mother Nature may be good at mixing races, but she would have had a hard time getting that lot together! My neighbor on the right here, and on the following pages, is a genuine show biz glamour puss.

ABOVE: Carragato Lassik, Gold Spotted California Spangled, belonging to Mrs. Vanna Maria Tatti.

RIGHT AND FOLLOWING PAGES: Tootsie, Non-Pedigree Cat, belonging to Mr. and Mrs. William Weldens.

MANX

The squat, rounded body of the Manx is accentuated by its distinguishing feature: its lack of tail! It is average-sized, muscular and compact (in technical terms, "cobby"). Its strong forelegs are shorter than its muscular hind legs, so its rump looks like that of a bear, or a rabbit... and some of these cats advance in leaps called "Manx Hops."

It has a rounded head, with a muzzle which is slightly longer than it is wide. It has prominent cheeks and a curved forehead. Its big, round eyes are set well apart, at a slight slant. Their color corresponds with that of the coat, which is silky with a

close, thick undercoat. Ideally, the Manx is "Rumpy," i.e., with a small, round rump and no tail at all. However, the gene responsible for this mutation is variable: certain cats, known as "Rumpy Risers," have up to three coccygeal vertebrae covered with a tuft of hair; others, called "Stumpies," have an embryo tail up to ten centimeters long. Some kittens are born with an almost normal-length tail; they are known as "tailed Manx," and only used for reproduction.

The Manx Cat, from the Isle of Man in the Irish Sea, is one of the oldest breeds of domestic cat. It attracted the attention of

British breeders in the early 1900s. Initially, cats that were born with too long a coat were rejected from the breeding program; in the 1960s, Americans began to take an interest in these scorned creatures, and used them to produce a new breed which they called "Cymric" (Welsh for "Wales"!).

Like the Manx, the Scottish Fold on the next pages also has a double, which is called the "Highland Fold" because of its fur. You will find it described on page 100, together with the Cymric, in the "Longhair" section.

Shen's Lady (ABOVE), Yuki and Winnie de la Gambade, Manx, belonging to Mrs. Huguette Noebels.

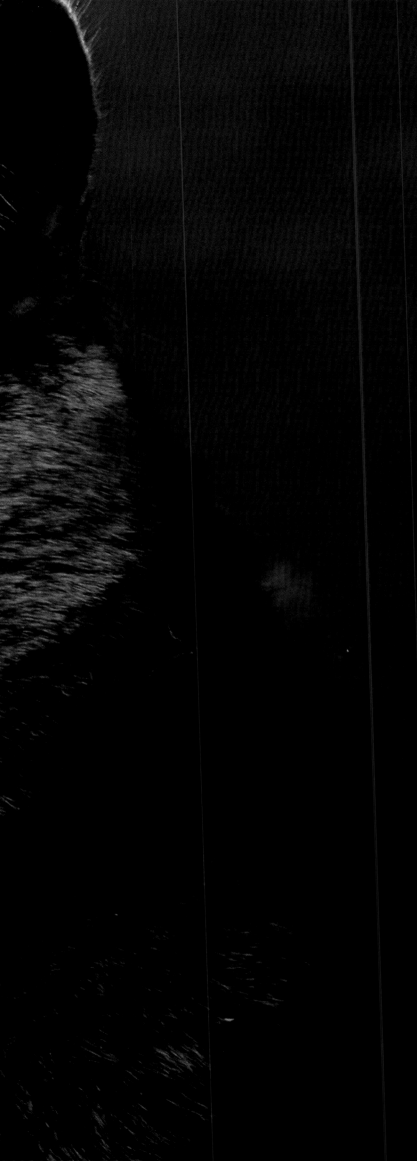

CHARTREUX

The Chartreux was made famous by French author Colette. This cat is a uniform blue-gray, the color of a stormy sky, including its nose leather and its pads. Its bright, deep yellow or copper-colored eyes stand out from this dark background. It is a strong, heavily built cat, with a broad chest and medium-length, powerful legs. It is distinguished from other Blues by the shape of its head, which is broad, rounded, and wider at the base with well-developed jowls (especially in male cats). There is a narrow, flat space between the ears, which are set high on the head, accentuating the distinctive shape of the head. The nose is broad and straight, without a stop. Another characteristic feature is its fur, which is thick and glossy, with a slightly woolly undercoat. The coat must be even in tone, without any tipping. There must be no highlights or markings of any kind, and no hint of green in the eyes.

PRECEDING DOUBLE PAGE:
Mar de Barret known as Liberty,
Van Black and White Scottish
Fold, and Scotland Yard, Black
Silver Classic Tabby and White
Van Scottish Fold, belonging to
Mrs. Yannick Prescott-Quefféléant.

LEFT AND ABOVE:
Darling du Sacré Cœur,
Chartreux, belonging to
Mrs. Marie-Lucie Malenovic.

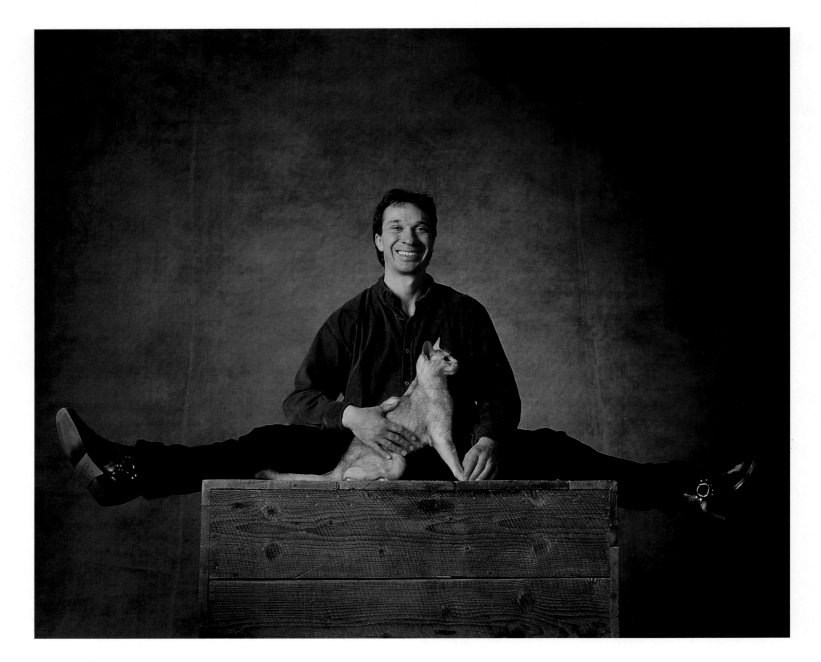

ABYSSINIAN

The first Abyssinian was brought back to Britain from Abyssinia (now Ethiopia) in 1868, by the members of a military expedition, who named the cat "Zula" after the port where they had arrived. The breed was fixed in Britain, where, in order to keep the distinctive features of the original (especially her "ticked" coat), she was mated with carefully chosen local shorthairs, as similar to her as possible. However, a photo of the original proves that she did not look much like her modern-day descendants.

In 1871 the Abyssinian was presented at the first cat show at the Crystal Palace in London. In 1889, the first Standard of Points for the breed was published, and in 1926, the Abyssinian Cat Club was formed in England. The following year, the breed appeared in France, in the shape of a certain British-born "Ras Tafari."

It soon became extremely popular, and breeding programs were set up all over Europe and America, where today it is one of the most popular breeds, along with Siamese and Persians. It is true that the Abyssinian is an exceptionally elegant cat, reminiscent of an Egyptian divinity.

Its body is medium-sized, supple and muscular, with a long, tapering tail. It has long, slim legs with visible tendons, and small oval feet. Its head is triangular, with gently rounded, harmonious contours. It has a firm chin, a medium-sized nose and quite large rounded ears, which are usually furnished on the inside. Its large, almond-shaped eyes are circled with a dark line. They must be set well apart, and pure gold, green or amber in color. The coat is short, fine and closelying, with the characteristic two or three dark bands of ticking, the tips being preferably dark. Whether the coat color is ruddy, sorrel, blue, fawn or silver, there must be no markings on the chest, belly or legs. The nose leather, pads, and sometimes the tip of the tail must correspond to certain criteria, depending on the coat color.

ABOVE AND FOLLOWING PAGES:
Diamond Silver d'Altaïr
of Cinnamon's,
Sorrel Silver Abyssinian,
belonging to Mr. Gilles Guillaumes.

CATS
AND TIGERS (1)

The poet Paul Valéry wrote of the tiger in the London Zoo: "It is not possible to be more oneself, more perfectly educated, endowed and equipped with all that is necessary to be a perfect tiger. The tiger feels no appetites or temptations which it can not instantly satisfy. I would give it this motto: FORTHRIGHTNESS."

(to be continued)

Hot Shot Lone Star, Fiona Lone Star, Hennessy Lone Star and Shechinah Esprit d'Amour, Ruddy Abyssinians, belonging to Mrs. Daniela Goll.

CATS
AND TIGERS (2)

Moncrif had similar comments to make about the cat: "master of its situation... its skill and its sobriety are so many guarantees of a pleasant future," and: "their agility and their claws are all their wealth, all their world."...
(to be continued)

ABOVE: Gennetic's Black Silver d'Alyse de la Pagerie, Black Silver Abyssinian, belonging to Mrs. Alyse Brisson.

RIGHT: Helwétia de Fontanalbe, Fawn Abyssinian, belonging to Mrs. Marie-Louise Giraud.

CATS
AND TIGERS (3)

Victor Hugo's cat inspired Joseph Méry to declare: "God made the cat to give man the pleasure of caressing the tiger"... a natural conclusion, if one compares Paul Valéry's reaction to the tiger with Moncrif's description of the cat.

Bahariya's Tefnout Blue Genes (ABOVE), Blue Abyssinian, and Zazie, Bi-Color European, belonging to Mr. Claude Paul Godenir and Mr. Marcel Godenir.

HEAVEN SCENT

Behavioral science teaches us that when the cat rubs so lovingly against us, it is only in order to exchange scents. In a sense, it claims us as its plaything… and what's more, it obviously revels in the process!

Cinnamon's Fersen,
Sorrel Abyssinian,
belonging to Mr. Franck Massé.

LONGHAIR

CATS

THE ABYSSINIAN AND ITS DOUBLE, THE SOMALI

*T*he Somali is African in name rather than in origin, as it is simply a longhaired version of the Abyssinian. This natural mutant appeared in the 1930s, but was excluded from breeding programs for a long time because of its fur, and it was not until the 1960s that American breeders took an interest in it. Nowadays, it is universally recognized; it conforms to the same Standard as the Abyssinian, except for the length of its coat—which forms breeches and a ruff, but has the same ticking.

ABOVE: Lynn Lee's Black Eyed Susan.
RIGHT: Lynn Lee's Secret Wishes, Ruddy Somalis, belonging to Mr. and Mrs. Alain Piette.

A MAGYAR'S MUSTACHE

In the late nineteenth century, the cat was becoming a fashionable pet. A reference work was devoted to our feline friend by French author Jules Husson (writing as "Champfleury"), a friend of Baudelaire, Courbet and Nadar. The cover was illustrated by Edouard Manet, and many of the great names of the time feature in its pages as (sometimes unexpected) cat-lovers.

The book is a pleasant combination of history and legend, art and literature, dotted with personal reflections and anecdotes. We discover, for example, that when Champfleury was a young man he had the singular honor of being received in Victor Hugo's Gothic drawing-room by the feline master of the house: "In the middle of the room, there was a large red canopy. There a cat sat enthroned, apparently waiting to accept visitors' tributes. A huge collar of white fur stood out from its black coat like a chancellor's cape; it had the mustache of a Hungarian Magyar, and when the animal advanced solemnly towards me, looking at me with its blazing eyes, I realized that the cat had modeled itself on the poet, and reflected the great thoughts that filled the dwelling." Maybe this beautiful Ruddy Somali with its imposing mustache sometimes dreams that, during one of its nine lives, it once had Victor Hugo for master?

ABOVE: Lynn Lee's Secret Wishes.

RIGHT AND FOLLOWING DOUBLE PAGE: Hyacinth des Fauve et Or, Blue Somali, belonging to Mrs. Christine Le Renard.

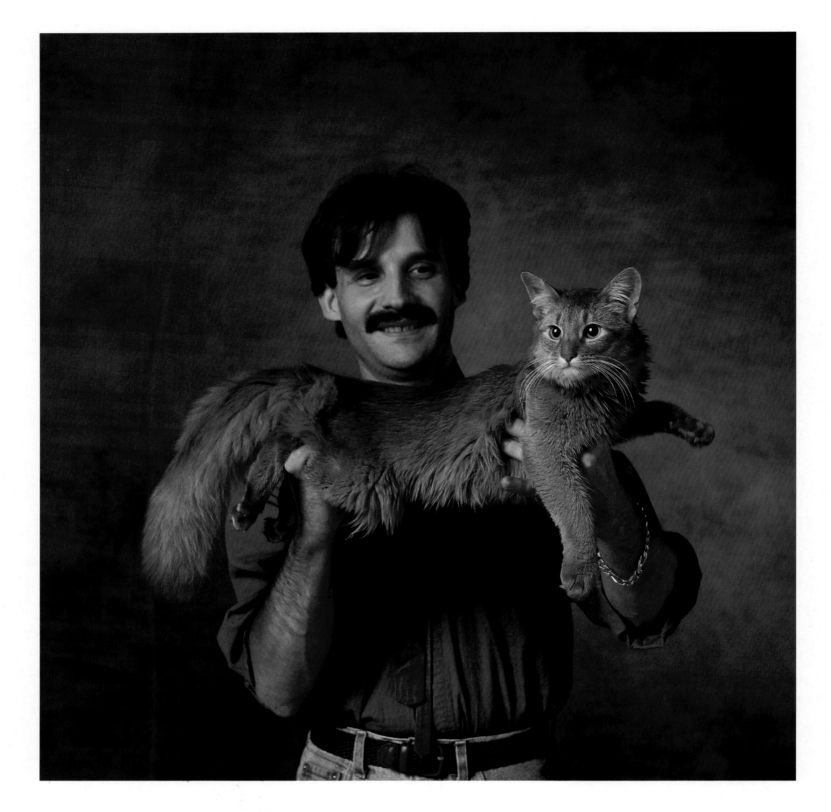

KINGS AND JESTERS

Poets may wax lyrical with their "Chancellor's capes," "Magyar's mustaches" and "great Sphinxes, stretched out in the desert of solitude"... but the cat pays no attention and often has no time for grandeur and dignity. So it can often be seen boxing invisible flies, hunting imaginary prey in the folds of a rug or chasing its victims' shadows. When in a stately mood, however, it may deign to be entertained by the antics of its human court jesters.

Helie-Tim du Bois Galant, known as Heliot, Sorrel Somali, belonging to Mr. Patrick-Michael Reygner.

SCOTTISH CATS

Like the Manx and the Cymric, the Scottish and the Highland Fold Cat are the result of a spontaneous mutation. In their case, it took place in Scotland in the 1960s. They are the same in all respects except for the length of their fur. They are rather short-bodied cats, with a particularly rounded appearance: they have medium-length legs with round paws, a rounded chest and body, and a rounded head. With their folded ears and big round eyes, they look a bit like owls. It seems that the mutant gene responsible for these curious folded ears is also the cause of bone problems; so the

Folds are regularly mated with other breeds, to keep them healthy... all round!

HEADS OR TAILS?

The taillessness of the Manx and Cymric cats has given rise to all manner of legends. It is said, for example, that the cat from the Isle of Man was the last to enter Noah's Ark, and that the closing door severed its tail. Or that invading soldiers cut off the cats' tails to adorn their helmets, until the mother cats decided to deprive these barbarians of their trophies by nipping off their own

kittens' tails... and finally only tailless kittens were born. In a less poetic legend, the Manx Cat is said to be the result of secret matings with rabbits!

Throughout the ages, the tip of the cat's tail has electrified the human imagination. In Japan, the lucky Bobtail Cat has its unlucky counterpart, the evil "Nekomata," with a tail that splits in two, giving it the power to change into a female vampire or bloodthirsty demon. In the same vein, it used to be thought in Brittany that the cat's tail contained the power that enabled it to change into a witch... so naturally it was cut off, to avoid any

trouble! Sometimes a tom cat's ears were cut off, so that it would be too ashamed to go and join the devil—or maybe it was simply so that it would stay at home and chase mice, instead of indulging in its usual Tom-foolery!

ABOVE: H2o de Cour Saint-Eloi, Tortoiseshell Cymric, belonging to Ms. Florence Prescott.

RIGHT: Hidole des Sentiers Sauvages, Highland Fold, belonging to Mr. and Mrs. Christian Doublet-Picroyer.

NORSK SKOGKATT   NORWEGIAN FOREST CAT

HEAR NO EVIL

*T*he sturdy-looking Norsk is a big, powerfully built cat with a long body. Its muscular hind legs are slightly longer than its front legs, and it has big round paws with tufts between the toes. Its head forms an equilateral triangle, tipped with long, straight, wide-open ears, which are set high on the head and well-furnished with fur inside; ideally, they also have lynx-like tufts at the tips. The chin must be very firm, and the profile absolutely straight, with no trace of a stop at the base of the forehead. The large, slightly slanting eyes can be of any color, regardless of the color of the coat, which can itself be any color except chocolate and lilac, and have any markings except pointed patterns. The cat carries its long, bushy tail proudly aloft; when it is laid back along its body, it should reach to its neck. Its semi-long fur is double, with a woolly undercoat, and a long, smooth, water-resistant outer coat on its back and sides. In winter, the cat has a full shirt front, breeches and side whiskers; but after the annual moult, only the tail remains bushy.

*T*his magnificent young lady, with her tail draped so elegantly around her, is completely deaf. That is the unfortunate price she pays for having a pure white coat and heavenly blue eyes.
For genetic reasons, white cats with blue eyes are usually more or less deaf. The only exception to this rule is the Foreign White, which is in any case an exceptional creature, as it can be classified both white Siamese and blue-eyed Oriental Shorthair.

Naima's Yacinta, White Norwegian Forest Cat (Norsk Skogkatt), belonging to Mrs. Theres Ramseyer.

ORIGINS

Despite its name, the Norwegian Forest Cat is no relation to *Felis Sylvestris,* the European Wild Cat, which used to be unknown in Scandinavia. We know from Norse mythology that the Skogkatt had long been established there: the chariot of Freya, goddess of love, was drawn through the sky by a pair of these magnificent creatures.

In 1746, the Swedish naturalist Linnaeus, one of the founders of modern natural history, was the first to suggest that the domestic cat had exotic origins. No doubt he was familiar with the Skogkatt, which at that time lived semi-wild in the woods or was a working farm cat. Nowadays we think the Vikings probably introduced the Skogkatt into Scandinavia in the eighth century to kill rats, and that it originates from the banks of the Caspian Sea. Its solid, rugged appearance and its thick watertight coat would then be the result of its gradual adaptation to the climate.

In the 1930s, Norwegian breeders became interested in preserving the originality of their local farm cat, which was threatened with crossbreeding on account of growing enthusiasm for other breeds. The first Standard of Points was fixed in Norway in 1972; five years later, the Skog-

katt was internationally recognized. In order to maintain the features that distinguish it from other Northern long-haired cats and to avoid "fakes," the only "Norsk Skogkatts" that may be shown are those with a pedigree, and the "novice" category is forbidden for this breed.

Hanske de la Cachouteba,
Blue Tabby and White Norwegian
Forest Cat (Norsk Skogkatt),
belonging to Mrs. Christine Pochez.

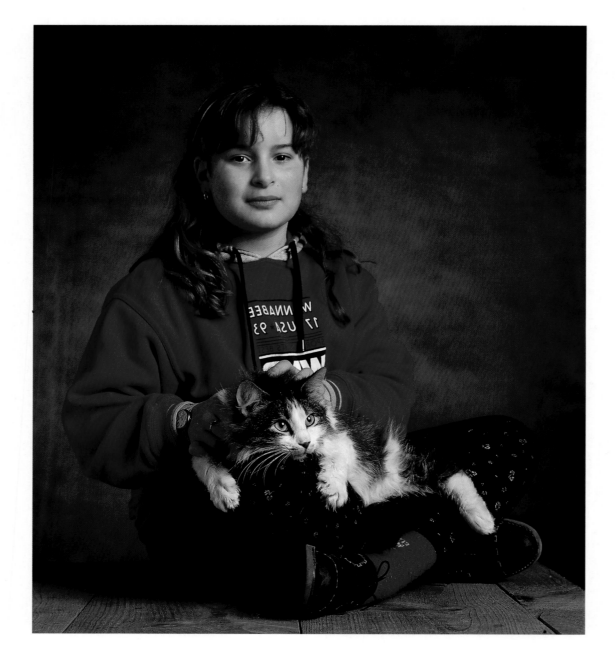

SIBERIAN FOREST CAT

In 1990, the Siberian Forest Cat came West, but it had already been bred in East Germany and Czechoslovakia for some years. Now that there is greater interest in the cat in Russia itself, a birth registry has been started at the official club in St. Petersburg.

It's a sturdy, powerfully built creature—males can weigh over ten kilos and females around six. It has a massive body with a solid bone structure, a very muscular back, shoulders and sides, and a broad, straight chest. Its legs are of medium-length; its large, slightly oval paws have little tufts of fur between the toes.

Its tail is shorter than that of the Norwegian Forest Cat, but is strong and thick, covered in same-length hairs implanted perpendicularly from the base right to the rounded tip.

Its head forms a rounded triangle, with a wide forehead, high cheekbones and small, full cheeks. Its large, wide-open eyes are almond-shaped, set wide apart and slightly slanting. Its medium-sized ears are broad at the base, gently rounded towards the tips, with pretty wisps of long hair along the inner edges. They are set well to the sides of the head, and tilt slightly forward.

The double coat consists of a thick undercoat and a rougher, water-repellent top coat. It is particularly spectacular in winter, with its breeches and superb ruff, which starts at the cheeks and partly covers the front legs. All coat colors are allowed, with a preference for "agouti" (coats with alternating light and dark areas).

This cat is a good climber and hunter, but a calm and reserved household pet. Siberian peasants probably used it as a guard-cat, because it has a tendency to growl at the approach of strangers.

Horacio des Loricaria of Siberia, Agouti and White Siberian Forest Cat, belonging to Mrs. Micheline Bancarel.

MAINE COON

The Maine Coon is a true American cat, which owes its name to its state of origin, and to the raccoon! According to legend, it is the result of matings between the little masked mammals and local cats running wild in the forests. More seriously, it no doubt resulted from spontaneous crossbreeding between local shorthaired farm cats, introduced by the first pioneers, and Angoras imported by New England sailors.

This hypothesis is the most likely, but as it is not proven, those who hanker after more romantic versions are free to believe the following story: Marie-Antoinette gave her Angora cats to the Marquis de Lafayette when he was leaving for the War of Independence, and when the Royal Cats arrived in the New World, they forgot their noble origins and mingled with the local population... Whatever the truth of its origins, the Maine Coon was a pioneer at American cat shows and was a great success at Madison Square Garden in 1895.

Its fortunes began to decline in the early 1900s however, with the arrival of more "exotic" cats like the Persian and the Siamese, and it was not until the 1950s that breeders renewed their interest in it and it returned to favor. It is a sturdy, medium to large cat, with a long, rectangular body. Its well-proportioned legs are strong and muscular, and it has big round paws with tufts between the toes. Its head is large, with high cheekbones, a medium-long nose and a strong chin. Its eyes are set well apart, on a slight slant; they may be any color. Its large, pointed ears are set high on its head and well-furnished inside. It has a long, luxuriant, plumed tail. Its silky fur falls smoothly, but is shorter and more close-lying on its head and shoulders; the fine undercoat is covered with a glossy, slightly oily, protective coat. As with the Norsk Skogkatt, all colors are permitted, except chocolate, lilac and Siamese Points.

Rexotic Gary, Brown Classic Tabby Maine Coon, belonging to Mr. Denis Basile.

Black magic

"Black in the night. Blacker than the night. Blacker than a brawl in a cellar at midnight. I don't need to hide in order to disappear; I simply cease to exist, and I switch off my headlamps. But I can do better still: I place my golden headlamps near the carpet, where they float in midair, visible but elusive... and I go about my business."

COLETTE, *Other Beasts*

Hindi of Kamloof,
Black Maine Coon,
belonging to Mr. Gérard Beroud.

TURKISH CATS

The first specimens of Turkish Angora cats were taken to Italy in the seventeenth century by the explorer Pietro della Valle. This breed originated on the high plateaus of the Middle East, and owes its name to the city of Ankara (previously spelt Angora). It contributed greatly to the development of the Persian, but then began to die out, overshadowed by the greater popularity of its rival. It was even threatened by crossbreeding in its country of origin, and was saved just in time thanks to a breeding program imposed on Ankara Zoo by the Turkish government.

In 1959, it was rediscovered by a visiting American breeder. The Turkish Angora is strong, solidly built but graceful, with long legs and small round paws with tufts between the toes. It has a triangular head, and large, pointed, high-set ears with pretty wisps of fur inside. Its eyes are almond-shaped and slightly slanting, and it has a medium-length nose without a stop. Its bushy tail is long and tapering, and must be carried low. Its semi-long coat is fine and silky, without an undercoat; the adult cat has a ruff.

The Turkish Van is very similar to the Turkish Angora. It also comes from a native Turkish population in the region of Lake Van, where it was discovered by British breeders in the 1960s. It is known as the "Swimming Cat" because of its fondness for water. Its body is pure white, but it is distinguished by the auburn color of its forehead and the top of its head, and its tail is similarly colored, with faint ring-markings.

It has pale amber, pink-rimmed eyes; its nose leather, the insides of its ears and its pads are also pink. Breeders are working on fixing its marking, in a variety of colors.

*Gaëtan le Fétiche des Loricaria,
Cream and White
Turkish Angora, belonging to
Mrs. Micheline Bancarel.*

CAT-WOMAN

As Léonor Fini pointed out: "With *die Katze*, German is the only language that expresses the feminine nature of the species as a whole—because cats are in fact females. The female cat is the exemplary, primordial cat, as the English language confirms, by referring to the male of the species as a 'Tom cat', as if the generic name was the female's prerogative." From ancient Egypt to Japan, from antiquity to the present day, whatever its grammatical gender, the cat symbolizes femininity.

Goufy de la Belle Blanche of de la Perle d'Antalya, Fany, Hendjyie (ABOVE), Houchka de la Perle d'Antalya, Turkish Angoras, belonging to Mr. and Mrs. Jean Bernel.

OF CATS
AND WOMEN

Bastet, the ancient Egyptian cat-goddess of love, fertility, mother-hood and childhood, reigned over an essentially female do-main. Freya, the Norse goddess of love, was portrayed arriving on a chariot drawn by white cats. She-devils, harpies and other feline creatures could meta-morphose into cats—females of course—or panthers. Popular tra-dition, beginning in Renaissance Naples and spreading through-out Europe, associates the cat with female genitalia, and com-mon speech attests to this. This widespread association no doubt originates in the traditional prox-imity of woman and cat: the cat stays at home with its mistress, while the dog goes off hunting with its master. On frescoes found in Theban tombs, women are shown at their dressing-tables under the watchful eye of tame cats wearing collars or leashes. Egyptian pots of kohl, tubes, perfume bottles, mirrors and jewelry were often deco-rated with the effigies of cats. The animal itself became asso-ciated with the beauty of those who tried to resemble it: Cleo-patra boasted of having an ideally feline form. The cat's natural elegance and its elabo-rate personal grooming habits have no doubt contributed to the fact that it is linked symbolically with woman. This might be seen as harmless vanity, but if we also consider its sensuality, its fond-ness for being caressed and for stretching out voluptuously in the sun, then the creature turns into the evil temptress of Christian imagery—although the mother cat is an irreproachable ex-ample of maternal care and domestic virtue.

_____

*PRECEDING DOUBLE PAGE AND
RIGHT: Hadjan de Capoutan-Lidj,
White and Auburn Turkish Van,
belonging to Mrs. Maryse Mayoux.*

RAGDOLL

The Ragdoll is a big strong cat, with semi-long fur, deep blue eyes, and the point markings of a Siamese. Sometimes it has white mitts like those of the Birman, and it can be Bi-color when all its paws are white and it has a white inverted 'V' on its forehead. It is called Ragdoll be-cause it's a gentle giant, which relaxes so completely when it's held that it goes quite floppy! It is appreciated by the public for this "floppiness," which makes it exceptionally docile and cuddly, although it's a quality that varies from one Ragdoll to another. No serious scientific study to date has determined the reason for this, and although this feature is sup-posed to characterize the cat, it is not included in its current Stan-dard of Points. Legend has it that the first Ragdolls were born to a cat that had been hit by a car; they were floppy due to ante-natal trauma and passed on their limpness to their own offspring. But this story is genetically impos-sible: trauma is not a transmit-table gene. It is therefore more likely that the Ragdoll simply inherited this quality from the placid Persian and gentle Bir-man which contributed, along with the Siamese, to its creation.

LEFT: *Bag-of-Rags Melissa,*
ABOVE AND RIGHT: *Pandapaws*
Eddie,
RIGHT: *Jonathan de Cyanara,*
Ragdolls, belonging to
Mrs. Vanna Maria Tatti.

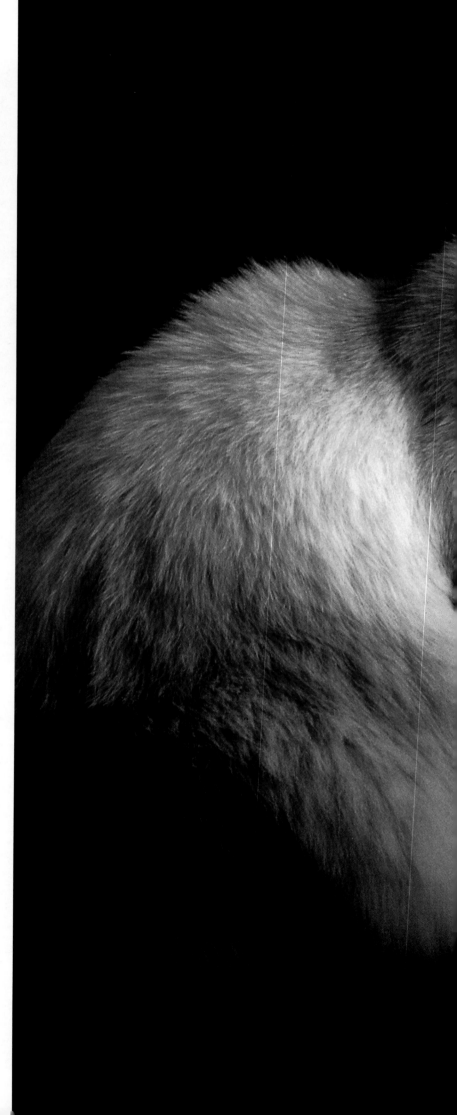

SACRED CAT OF BURMA

The Birman, or Sacred Cat of Burma, has a long, strong-boned body with short, powerful legs. The male is stockier than the female, but must not have the compact shape of a Persian. Its head is broad and round, with full cheeks, a strong chin, a medium-length nose and a gently curving forehead. Its ears are quite small and set at a slant. Its deep blue eyes are almost round. The coat is silky, without much undercoat; it is long on the back and sides, short on the legs and face, with a full ruff beginning at the cheeks. The chest and belly are a pale eggshell color, the back is a golden fawn, and the coat has the Siamese pointed pattern, together with the characteristic "mitts" and "socks." The toes are a pure white color that extends over the tops of the paws, but must not extend too far, or go up the sides of the legs. Ideally, the marking should be the same on all four paws; but the rear paws may have a larger white area than the fore paws, provided the markings on left and right legs are symmetrical.

---

*Fol Amour (ABOVE) and
Henessy de la Perle d'Or,
Seal Point Birmans,
belonging to Mrs. Nicole Godier.*

The Birman arrived in France in 1919, brought from its homeland by Auguste Pavie and Major Gordon Russell, who had been given a pair of these cats. The male cat did not survive the journey, but the female soon produced a litter of kittens which became the founders of an extremely well-loved breed, which was recognized in France in 1925, but almost disappeared during World War II.

Thanks to the efforts of French breeders, the Birman was saved, and was back in fashion in the 1950s. It arrived in the United States in the early 1960s, and was recognized in Great Britain in 1966 as the "Sacred Cat of Burma," in order to avoid any confusion with the Burmese, which has the same geographical origin but is otherwise quite different.

ABOVE: Gentiane de la Perle d'Or, Blue Point Birman, belonging to Mrs. Nicole Godier.

RIGHT: Filibert, Seal and Blue Birman, belonging to Mrs. Pascale Richard.

A SACRED CAT

To thank Auguste Pavie and Major Gordon Russell for helping them to escape, persecuted monks are said to have given them a pair of Birmans. This gift had all the more value as these cats had been considered sacred since the day one of them had saved the temple of Lao-Tsun… and changed color!

It was at the beginning of the eighteenth century. In the temple dedicated to Tsun-Kyankse, the sapphire-eyed goddess who presides over the transmigration of souls (and could order the reincarnation of priests in the body of cats) the venerable high priest Mun-Ha sat meditating with his faithful companion Sinh, a white, golden-eyed cat, whose nose, ears, legs and tail were the color of earth, a symbol of impurity. When pillagers approached the temple that moonlit night, the sage began to die before the very eyes of the horrified priests. Sinh leapt straight onto its master's head, and remained frozen there, facing the statue of Tsun-Kyankse.

As its master died, the bristling fur on its back suddenly turned a golden color, its eyes became as blue as those of the goddess, and its paws, which were touching its elderly master's white hair, changed from brown to purest white. It then turned toward the temple's southern doorway, and the priests, spurred into action by this miracle, rushed to close the heavy bronze doors, thereby saving the temple from pillage and profanation. Sinh stayed with his master for seven days and refused all food; then he too died, taking the soul of Mun-Ha to the goddess. The time came to choose his successor; before the assembled priests, the hundred temple cats appeared: they had all undergone the same transformation as Sinh. On their silent, white-gloved paws, they approached the youngest priest, and gazed at him with their sapphire eyes, indicating that he had been chosen by Tsun-Kyanske.

When a sacred cat dies at the temple of Lao-Tsun, it is the soul of a priest which returns to take its rightful place in paradise.

PRECEDING DOUBLE PAGE:
Hermès de Song-Hio,
Red Point Birman,
belonging to Mrs. Brigitte Rozet.

Hirondelle, Seal Tortie Point
Birman, belonging to
Mrs. Brigitte Rozet.

BALINESE

The similarity of their colors makes it likely that Birmans, Balinese and Siamese once had common ancestors in the Far East. But whereas the sacred cat, with its snowy paws, small ears and fairly heavy body, came from Burma in the early 1900s, the Balinese appeared unexpectedly in litters of ordinary Siamese in the 1940s. Its consequent development was very similar to that of the Somali, a mutant Abyssinian with semi-long fur: initially it was excluded from reproduction because of its "defective" fur, but ended up attracting attention to itself, and having specific breeding programs devoted to it, to preserve its Siamese qualities: its elongated, angular body and colorpointed coat pattern.

Alegrías Casa Decano of
la Draiecour and her kittens,
Blue Tabby Balinese, belonging to
Mr. and Mrs. Serge Ferenczi.

CREATING THE CAT

The Balinese and the Mandarin have identical morphology, which is similar in every way to that of the Orientals and Siamese shown in detail in the next chapter. But although the Balinese, a longhaired Siamese breed "fixed" in the 1970s, has been internationally recognized for a decade, the longhaired Oriental is still being perfected by breeders.

Called Mandarins, the specimens which correspond to the desired standard are crossed with Balinese for the "longhair" gene, with Orientals for their color, or even with Siamese, to the annoyance of purists. These crossings usually result in mixed litters, with a hotch-potch of Balinese, Mandarins and surprise kittens. The kittens that do not conform to the standards of either breed are called "variants"; they still have a perfectly legitimate pedigree, as well as the required morphology. They have genes which are potentially useful to fix the new breed, and represent an inevitable transitional stage. Even if they cannot be shown, they are used for reproduction. One day there will be enough authentic Mandarins for them to be mated together without too great a risk of inbreeding, and the resulting kit-

tens will all—or almost all—be Mandarins.

Pride and Freesia Casa Decano of la Draiecour, Blue Tabby and Chocolate Tabby Balinese, belonging to Mr. and Mrs. Serge Ferenczi.

Gatz'Arts de la Draiecour,
Lavender Mackerel Tabby Mandarin,
belonging to
Mr. and Mrs. Serge Ferenczi.

SIAMESE

AND

ORIENTALS

Zissi of Tontuta,
Chocolate Point Siamese,
belonging to Mr. Jean-Louis Nicolet.

SIAMESE AND ORIENTALS

The Siamese and Oriental are both elegant creatures with a hint of the "Pink Panther" in their profile—perhaps the famous figure was modeled after them! They are identical in shape, but form two groups according to color. Firstly, the Oriental's eyes are as invariably green as those of the Siamese are blue; secondly, the color of the Oriental's coat— whatever it may be—is uniform over the body, whereas the Siamese has a different color pattern, known as "points," on its face, legs, ears and tail.

There is one notable exception: should the Foreign White be considered an all-white Siamese, or is it a dissident blue-eyed Oriental?

Siamese and Orientals are medium-sized cats; their supple, muscular bodies are slim and angular, and they have long, slender legs with small oval paws. The tail is long and fine, tapering to a point. The slender neck carries a triangular head, which widens out in straight lines from the nose; this triangle is extended by the large, pointed ears, which are wide at the base. A hollow-cheeked or "pinched" effect around the muzzle is not considered desirable. In profile,

Gengis Khan du Domaine Sacré, Foreign White Siamese, belonging to Mrs. Christiane Merckx.

the long, straight nose continues
the line of the slightly convex
forehead without a break. The
almond-shaped eyes are slightly
slanting, in perfect harmony with
the triangles formed by the nose,
head and ears.

If we look at cat magazines from
the 1970s, we see that the Siamese used to be less "pointed"

and angular than it is today,
proving that taste in cats evolves
too, and that esthetic research
plays an important part in the
selection work done by breeders.

_____

Amadeus of the Sweet Cats,
Blue Siamese,
belonging to Mrs.. Jacqueline Pierre.

A CAT'S KISS

On any street corner, in any park or garden, when cat meets cat they may decide to get to know each other better. So they get close and sniff noses in a sort of Eskimo kiss, sealing a pact of feline friendship. But when their human masters dare to do the same before their very eyes, they look away, as if offended. Is their pride hurt? Is their sense of decency outraged? Are they jealous? Whatever the reason, their lips are sealed.

Amadeus of the Sweet Cats and
Hugo de la Pergola, Seal Point Siamese,
belonging to Mrs. Jacqueline Pierre.

SIAMESE

"'Sacred cat! Cat of Siam! Royal cat!...' Easily said. But they only feed me rice and fish. Fish is a good thing. But always fish and rice, rice and fish... Do they think my Siamese origins, or perhaps my religion, forbid me to eat like anybody else? ... A dead jay—now the mere thought of that makes my mouth water... A slightly high, black and yellow salamander... so much more inspiring than that pale fish and that ghostly white rice."

COLETTE, *Other Beasts*

Hugo de la Pergola

MORE OF THE SAME

"It's true, I've eaten wood pigeons, a partridge, a tender rabbit... I was created to hunt all that is beige or fawn or brownish. Why else would the Master of All Things have given me this coat, the color of sand and dry leaves? But I'm only hidden as long as I keep my flame-blue eyes closed. As soon as I open them, everything flies away... Those little creatures are not up to such a blue."

COLETTE, *Other Beasts*

_____

Amadeus of the Sweet Cats.

PLAYING WITH FIRE

Behind its sky-blue gaze, Colette's princely Siamese dreams of devouring its prey, imagining perverse games: "For want of anything better, I shall test my wits against the only creature that dares look me in the eye, the one that ever since its fall has held a grievance against any-thing of a heavenly blue—my brother, the snake."

ABOVE: Rokon of Off, Lilac Point Siamese, belonging to Mr. Jacky Letourneau.
RIGHT: Farouk de la Rouvière, Chocolate Tabby Siamese, belonging to Mr. Louis Coste.

PORTRAIT

Soft and gentle cat-caress,
Snarling scratching cat-tigress,
Cat-goddess, protect from harm,
Temptress of grace and charm,
Free spirit, rest in my embrace,
Soft fur so close against my face,
Then turn your back, and go
your way...
A cat has other games to play!

*H'Isis du Domaine Sacré,
Seal Tortie Tabby Siamese,
belonging to
Mrs. Christiane Merckx.*

The symbolism of the Egyptian cat

The ancient Egyptian cat-goddess Bastet was associated with life-giving warmth and fertility. In contrast, her lion-headed sister Sekhmet was the goddess of destructive fire and war. But Bastet had originally been a lioness too, and the two sisters may simply be two sides of the same coin. According to legend, the sun-god Râ wanted protection against snakes, and sent the baboon-god Thoth to bring Bastet back from the Nubian desert where she was in hiding in the shape of a lioness. On the way home, she bathed in the Nile, and assumed the form of a cat; she then continued her jour-ney to Bubastis, "city of cats," which became the headquarters of her cult in 950 B.C. Bastet was goddess of motherhood, of childhood and then of the Egyptian people as a whole. She had power over the sun, and life itself: she protected the chest in which Osiris was thrown into the Nile by his ene-mies, and she was initiated into the mysteries of Atum, the "Great Cat," which killed the evil serpent Apophis every night when it threatened Râ's barge as it sailed through the underworld. So, in the Egypt of the Pharaohs, the cat was closely linked to the cycle of life, death and rebirth.

In the Egyptian "Book of the Dead," it was directly associated with the birth of Osiris, solar symbol of this same cycle. The god, son of Nut, goddess of the primordial sky, said this: "Born of the Cat, I am the chief, the son of the Cat, the double-guide, who will always be for his mother the little one who was rescued by the Cat."

Enki de l'Ile des Ravageurs,
Brown Spotted Tabby Oriental,
belonging to Mrs. Liliane Lesongeur.

BAUDELAIRE'S CAT

"He is the familiar spirit of the place;
He judges, presides, and in-
spires
All things within his empire;
Perhaps he is a fairy, perhaps he
is a god?"

        CHARLES BAUDELAIRE,
           Flowers of Evil

Gaodi de la Rouvière,
Lavender Oriental,
belonging to Mr. Louis Coste.

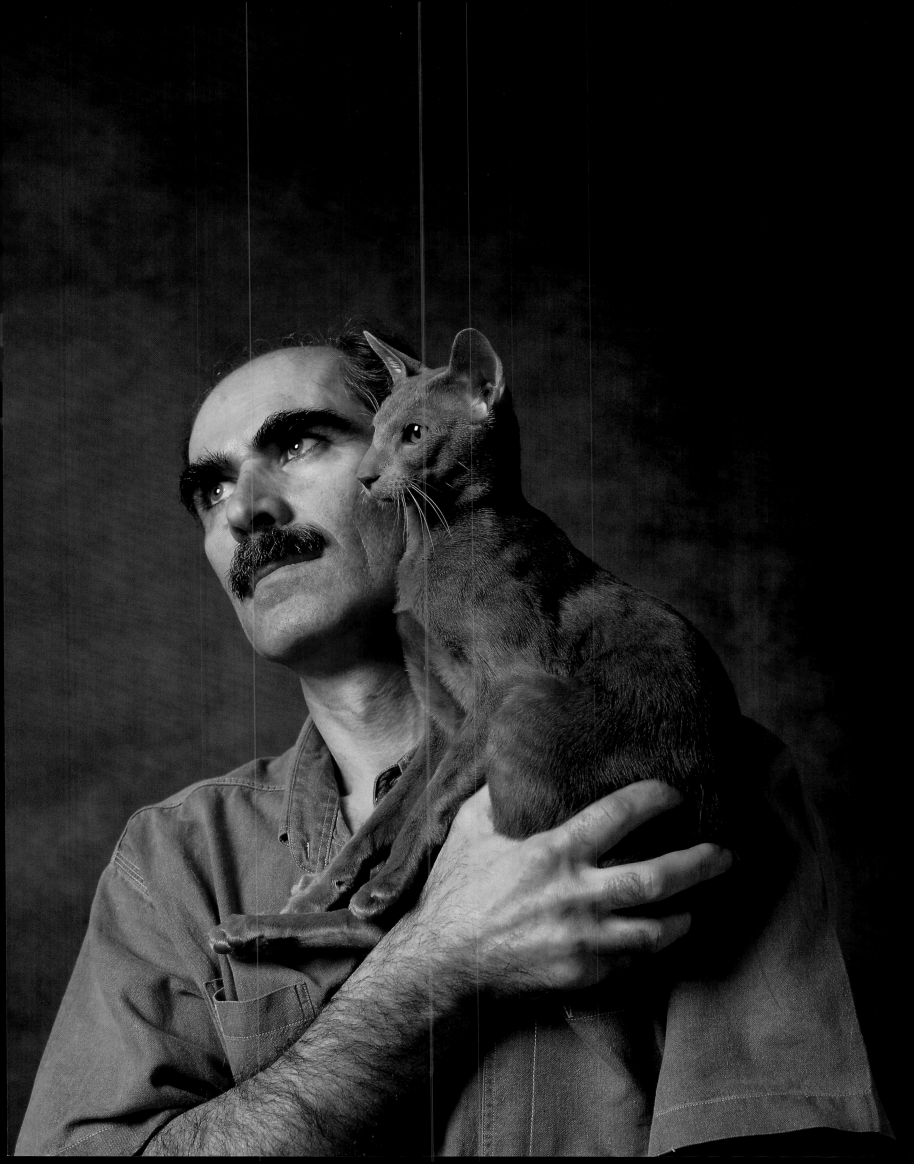

PRINCE OF DRAKNESS

"I am the devil. The devil. There can be no doubt about it. You only have to look at me. Go on, look at me—if you dare! Black— a black that's been singed by the fires of Gehenna. Poison-green eyes... I have horns... and claws, claws, claws. How many claws? I don't know. A hundred thousand perhaps... And beware, if I sing too loud tonight, of showing yourself at the window: you might be struck dead to see me, on the rooftop, showing black against the moon!..." This was Poum, Colette's cat.

The black cat is frightening. In the middle ages, it was thought to be the devil incarnate, and even to- day it is supposed to bring bad luck in our so-called civilized countries.

In 1727, while Europe was still in the grip of feline dark ages, the avant-garde Moncrif made a brave attempt to reinstate the ill- loved creature, with some curious arguments: "Mother nature has always been most jealous of her black cats; it seems that she only lets us sight one from time to time in order to prove that she knows how to make them.... It is true that the color black does much harm to the cat in vulgar minds; it brings out the fire in their eyes, which is enough for them to be thought sorcerers at the least...

but on the other hand, for people of good sense, this same color, together with the animal's char- ming ways, likens it to those people come from Africa, whose dark complexion gives them a wild appearance, yet who, once they were masters of Spain, see- med only to have conquered it in order to introduce politeness and gallantry."

ABOVE: Hermès de la Malvoisine, Ebony Oriental, belonging to Mr. Alain Gilman.

RIGHT: Gavroche de la Clère, Chocolate Oriental, belonging to Mrs. Patrick Geslot.

ORIENTAL

"**T**o understand the cat, one must be essentially feminine and poetic"—at least, according to Champfleury. But in order to understand this delicate Oriental creature with its snake-like tail and its meditative air, perhaps one must be a prophet like Mohammed, who cut off the sleeve of his robe so as not to disturb his cat's sleep.

Fifty-Fifty de Sophisticats, Bi-Color Black and White Oriental, belonging to Mrs. Chantal Dormat (ABOVE), and Hillou des Albatres, Cream Tabby Oriental, belonging to Ms. Elisabeth Contet.

REBEL!

Held up like trophies by the scruffs of their necks! On the pedestal of its Egyptian statue, the outraged cat protests at such dishonor: "Have you seen Sekhmet, the lioness? Have you seen her yawning, world-weary? Howling at the rising moon, on a winter's night?"

ABOVE: Dandy de la Romandière, Blue Tabby Oriental. RIGHT: Dandy and Harald des Albatres

FOLLOWING DOUBLE PAGE: Red Tabby Oriental, belonging to Ms. Elisabeth Contet.

PERSIANS

MISTAKEN IDENTITY

"**O**h! what a pretty flower in the window! ... I don't mean the little poppies, I mean the flower at the bottom, the velvety, speckled one, with two glistening dewdrops, and big, white, pointed stamens... Oh sorry, I made a mistake: it isn't a flower, it's a cat."

COLETTE, *Other Beasts*

ABOVE: Geisha de la Lumière cendrée, Shaded Golden Persian, belonging to Mr. and Mrs. Robert Bonnin.

RIGHT: Gaspard de la Roizonne, Red Persian, belonging to Mrs. Elisabeth Kassis.

PERSIANS

Persian and Exotic Shorthair cats have the same "dense" morphology, and the same range of colorings. In both cases, the eyes, nose leather and pads must correspond to certain criteria, depending on the coat color. The two breeds are differentiated by their type of fur: the Persian has a long, thick, silky coat, with a ruff falling over its chest and shoulders; the Exotic Shorthair is a shorthaired version of the Persian, with very thick fur which stands out from its body and is slightly longer than that of the British Shorthair.

Both breeds are medium-sized to large, with a massive body, broad chest, and muscular back and shoulders. The legs are short and thick, with large round paws, preferably with tufts between the toes. The tail is short, bushy in the case of the Persian, and must be proportionate to the body.

The large, round face, lit up by big, round, pure-colored eyes, gives these cats a moon-like appearance.

The ears are small, set wide apart and low on the head; they are slightly rounded, and well-furnished with fur inside. The nose is small and short, without being turned-up, and there is a stop just between the eyes. The forehead is prominent, and the cheeks and chin are well-developed.

We can trace the origin of black or white longhaired cats called "Persians" back to the sixteenth century; the present-day Persian with its fantastic colors is a result of the work done by European and American breeders, who started developing it in the 1800s, using ever-stricter selection procedures to adapt its colors to changing tastes.

The Exotic Shorthair, however— whose only exotic feature is its name—is a relatively recent cat. It did not acquire international recognition until 1984, but was created in the United States in the 1960s, from crossings between Persians and British or American shorthairs.

ABOVE: Gaïa and Geisha de la Lumière cendrée, Shaded Golden Persians, belonging to Mr. and Mrs. Robert Bonnin.

RIGHT: Garfield del Adène, Red Tabby Persian, belonging to Mrs. Danielle Espi

PERFECTING THE PERSIAN

The first longhaired Oriental cats introduced into Europe at the beginning of the seventeenth century were Turkish Angoras. In the eighteenth century, the Persian (Iranian) Angora made its appearance; it had thicker fur and a heavier body. By crossing the two breeds, then selecting, breeders obtained a type resembling our modern Persian: large and massive with small ears, a round head, and a short muzzle and nose. The type may still vary according to fashion, but the breed has been recognized since the first cat shows over a hundred years ago.

ABOVE: Sweet Mary dell'Ariette du Shah-Li, Brown Tabby and Black Persian, belonging to Mrs. Christiane Paillard.

RIGHT: Lilian Buissant des Amorie, Chinchilla Persian, belonging to Mr. and Mrs. Robert Bonnin.

CATS AND ROSES

Blue-cream, shaded silver, shell cameo, black smoke... the infinite variety of colors of the Persian's coat is a delight to ear and eye. Children's stories used to tell that when God had created the earth, the fairies came to color it. Today's fairies work in their secret laboratories, mixing miraculous colors on their palettes, dreaming up new cats as they dream up new roses.

Hermione de la Brakelière,
Blue-Cream and White Van Persian,
belonging to Mrs. Caroline Bonafos.

GESUNDHEIT!

In mythology, the cat is often associated with the lion. The Egyptian cat-goddess Bastet was sister and avatar of Sekhmet, the vengeful lioness. When the sun-god invented the lion, his sister Artemis made fun of him by creating the cat. And in Montesquieu's *Persian Letters*, he recounts the Islamic legend according to which the cat was born from the lion's nostrils: on the rat-infested ark, Noah was inspired by God to strike the lion on the forehead; the wild beast then sneezed out the first pair of cats, which rid the ark of its unwelcome guests.

H'Ormacif and Full-Ozass du Clos de Bagneux, Persians, belonging to Mrs. Marie-José Tirard.

THE CAT, THE SNAKE AND THE LION

In Egyptian mythology, the Great Cat Atum decapitated the evil snake Apophis every night, when it threatened the Sun's barge; and ever since, cat and snake have often been linked as enemies, rivals in their capacity as initiatory, fear-inspiring animals. But it is always the cat who triumphs over the snake... in a battle open to Freudian interpretation!

In his book *Black Cat, Mirror of Dreams,* Robert de Laroche tells how the only one of his pet cats that will chase a snake is the one born under the sign of "Leo"!

HIGH-CLASS RAT-CATCHER

In the early seventeenth century, Pietro della Valle imported the first longhaired Turkish cats into Italy; these were the ancestors of present-day Persians. Nicolas Claude Fabri de Peiresc, a councilor at the Aix parliament, did the same in France. Peiresc was an antique-dealer, collector, astronomer and naturalist, who happened to dislike European cats. He contributed a great deal to developing the breed of "beautiful cats from Ancyra or Angora." Whether he gave them to high dignitaries or exchanged them for valuable objects, he kept up with news of his protégés, and devised his own careful breeding program to keep the breed pure. His cats may have been magnificent creatures, but they were still ratters, as testified by a letter he wrote to the collector Borelli, dated January 31, 1631: "I am greatly obliged to these animals, which have delivered my books from the frequent attacks they used to suffer from rats."

Stardust dell'Ariette du Shah-Li, Tortoiseshell Persian, belonging to Mrs. Christiane Paillard.

PERSIAN PICNIC

Colombine de la Brakelière, Bi-Color Black and White Persian, belonging to Mrs. Yvette Framinet.

"**S**he's truly a Persian Shah, and it's easy to see that she's not from here. She grows very fast—in width rather than height—and is short-legged, agile and soft, with a plume of a tail as long as she is, low ears, a short, velvety nose... But certain musical sounds, certain muffled, barely perceptible noises terrify her, and her fur is all aghast and shimmering with nervous spikes... She is full of oriental superstition: two fingers held out like horns are enough to put her to flight... A very affected Shah, in short. A harem princess, with no dreams of escape. A very female, coquettish, prim and proper Shah, conscious of her beauty, which increases day by day. Was there ever a more magnificent Shah?"
On her first day in the country, the Shah disappeared. What would become of this delicate creature, which nibbles dainties from a China bowl? A search party hunted for her everywhere, from attic to cellar, in wood and field, up on the cliff top and down in the well. All hope seemed lost: alas, the Shah had vanished! And the searchers were on their way home to weep when, around a bend in the path, they came to a halt, hardly able to believe the sight that met their eyes: "In the middle of a circle of workmen having their lunch—among the clumpy mud-caked shoes, the trousers stiffened with plaster, the blue overalls, the faded caps—among the bottles of cider and cheap wine, the grease-stained papers and wooden-handled knives—perfectly at ease, smiling, tail held stiff as a candle and mustache at half-moon, amid the din of oaths and guffaws—the Shah, the divine Shah, full of cheese-rinds, rancid bacon and sausage skins, purrs, chases her plumed tail and plays at impressing the builders."

COLETTE,
The Peace of the Animals

174

CAT GOT YOUR TONGUE?

Our *Felis catus*, alias *domesticus*, has boasted a whole string of scholarly names, some of which it borrowed from other species. Ancient authors confused it with its fellow ratcatchers, the ferret, the marten and the weasel; medieval scholars called it *musio, muriceps, musipulus* or *murilegus*, all of which are variations derived from the name of its prey, *mus*, meaning "mouse."

In the fourth century, the word *catus* appeared for the first time, in the treatise on agronomy written by Palladius. The scholar Isidore of Seville deemed this Low Latin term vulgar, but it took hold nevertheless and is the origin of the cat's various European names: *chat, Katze, kot, gatto...* The origin of *catus* has scholars confounded (like the cat's secret name in T.S.Eliot's poem!): does it come from the Latin *captare* (to capture) or from *cattare* (to have keen eyesight), from *catus* (wise) or from *catulus* (puppy)? Or is it of African origin, from the Nubian *kadis*, from the Berber *kadiska*, from the Syrian *quatô* or the Arabic *qitt*, all of which mean "cat"? Or did *catus* colonize Africa?

To quote the poet again: "The naming of Cats is a difficult matter"!

PRECEDING DOUBLE PAGE AND ABOVE: Gina de la Brakelière, Blue-Cream and White Persian, belonging to Mrs. Sylviane Bourgois.

RIGHT: Geisha de la Brakelière, Harlequin Tortie and White Persian, belonging to Mr. and Mrs. Nicolas Georgeault.

ABOVE AND LEFT:
Hercule de la Brakelière,
Black and White Van Persian,
belonging to Mrs. Catherine Fromal.

RIGHT: Fedora de la Brakelière,
Tortie and White Persian,
belonging to Mrs. Sylviane Bourgois.

ETYMOLOGY

Ailurophobia" is the clinical term for the pathological fear of cats, which had ladies fainting in salons at the sight of the most innocent little feline, and is still widespread today.

Thanks to "ailurophilia," on the other hand, we are able to admire the beautiful cats shown on these pages, among many others. Medieval scholars chose to name the cat after its function as mouse-hunter, but the ancient Greeks were rather more poetic, and called it *ailouros:* the tail-waver.

Harmonie de l'Arc-en-ciel,
Red and White Van Persian,
belonging to Mrs. Catherine Fromal.

MAGIC WAND

The cat's tail helps ensure its physical balance and its mental equilibrium. When a cat stands at an open door and sees that it's pouring rain outside, it waves its tail frantically, indicating a state of conflict: do I go out and get wet, or do I stay indoors? When it finally decides, its tail stops wagging. It appears, therefore, that when a cat is prevented from a course of action by an unexpected contretemps, it "freezes," but the inhibited movement is transferred to its tail. This magical activity frees the cat from frustration, and allows it to decide with complete peace of mind.

TABLE MANNERS

"**C**ertain cooks are accustomed to sculpting scallops of butter with a knife, for lunch. By leaving a lump of butter within reach of the cat, the job can be done with greater expertise. With its rough tongue, it can draw very pretty flowers on the butter."

CHAMPFLEURY

Gamila de la Villouyère,
known as Cannelle,
Silver Tortie Tabby Persian, belonging
to Mrs. Françoise Vigneron.

FOOD, GLORIOUS FOOD!

"The average cat will eat just about anything that we will, and quite a few things that we won't... Fortunately, most cat-owners understand the role that a carefully planned diet plays in their cat's physical and emotional well-being. In addition to the usual fare, they provide their cats with such much-needed staples as asparagus, cheese, lobster, bread, pasta and strawberry shortcake. Knowing better than anybody else what's good for them, cats sometimes complete the menu with houseplants, goldfish, canaries, cigarettes and cigars, crayons, toothpaste,

wallpaper and dirty socks." Stephen Baker classifies the cat in the category (unknown to science) of "multi-omnivorous," and his humorous analysis of the cat's eating habits is not so far from the truth! One of my feline acquaintances adored watermelon peel and Russian dressing, and would beg for them at table like a dog, tearing at clothes and thighs in its desperation to get what it wanted. In the natural state, the cat is a flesh-eating predator... might contact with humans have perverted its tastes? The answer is no, because the cat is as naturally curious as it is carnivorous!

Eurydice Tresor de Bast,
Colorpoint Persian, belonging to
Mrs. Dominique Guérinaud.

AND NEVER THE TWAIN SHALL MEET

"Again I must remind you that A dog's a dog—a cat's a cat."

T. S. ELIOT

FAIRY TAILS

In 1682, Madame d'Aulnoy wrote a fairy-tale called *The White Cat,* in which a poor princess and her entire household are bewitched by wicked fairies. The princess is turned into a White Cat and, when a handsome prince falls in love with the beautiful creature, she tells him that he must cut off her head and tail and throw them into the fire in order to break the spell. The prince reluctantly agrees... and the Cat turns back into a beautiful princess. The prince marries her, and they live happily ever after. There is not such a happy ending, however, for the poor fellow in the fable by La Fontaine, who also manages to marry his beloved cat: but once a cat, always a cat... and on their wedding night, the Beauty suddenly interrupts their love-making to chase a passing mouse! The hero should no doubt have followed the example of the fairy-tale prince, and burned the cat's "bestial" characteristics... according to tradition, the cat represents woman, and the mouse represents man, so the moral of the tale becomes clearer!

The story of the cat metamorphosed into a woman was inspired by one of Aesop's fables. It was also the subject of one of Sergei Diaghilev's Russian ballets, which was performed in 1927 in Paris and Monte Carlo, to music by Henri Sauguet.

Houpette and Geisha
de la Charmeraie,
White Persians, belonging to
Mrs. Lysiane Chavallard.

THE CAT, THE HUNTER AND THE ASPARAGUS

Many of his contemporaries hated cats, but Champfleury was particularly irritated by the ailurophobia of Toussenel, a follower of the doctrines of Charles Fourier, who was also an ornithologist and hunter, and was certainly very virulent: "I never come across a marauding cat without doing it the honor of shooting at it.... I urge all my fellow hunters to do the same." That certainly sounds like prejudice against the poor creature!... but the fact is that, in the nineteenth century, the *Journal of Practical Agriculture* portrayed the cat as an unscrupulous and fanatical destroyer of all living

things: according to this publication, the perverse feline was constantly stuffed full of a multitude of hares, rabbits, partridges and nightingales, its sole aim in life being to deprive hunters of their pleasure and nature of its charms!

So it was up to Champfleury to defend the poor, scrappy, country cat, that only hunted in order to survive and remained obstinately thin despite these supposed orgies of game.

Moncrif's disciple was exasperated by Toussenel's stupidity rather than his cruelty, and reproached him for the absurdity of his complaints against the

cat—such as the fact that it likes asparagus, indisputable proof of its depraved tastes! "If we had to shoot at all the people who like asparagus, the population of France would soon be decimated. The cat likes the grasses that are necessary for its hygiene... He cannot find this greenery indoors, so is it not natural that he should wish, like his master, to taste flavorsome vegetables in the springtime? Such behavior hardly deserves gun shots."

PRECEDING DOUBLE PAGE AND ABOVE: Hermès de la Salamandre d'Or, Colorpoint Red Point Persian, belonging to Mr. Robert Lubrano.

RIGHT: Follow Me Ice Cube, Colorpoint Red Point Persian, belonging to Mr. Jean-Yves Ramel.

Bizarre, bizarre

In the story by Edgar Allen Poe, the Black Cat is a demon, sorcerer and symbol of guilt; a bristly Black Cat features on the sign designed by Théophile Steinlen for Rodolphe Salis's Montmartre cabaret; and sometimes it appears that the Black Cat does its best to live up to its curious reputation.

When I was living in London, I was adopted by a neighbor's black cat, which used to come in through my window on sunny days and make herself at home. Once, while she was curled up asleep on my bed, I began to listen to a recording of Verdi's Macbeth. To my amazement, she pricked up her ears as soon as the music began, and came to stand between the speakers, as still as an Egyptian statue, straining to hear. She kept this pose all through the record, looking at me impatiently when I had to turn it over. Then, when the opera was finished, she went back to sleep. And from that day on, whenever I put that record on she would appear as if by magic, begging to come in if the window was closed, and would take up her pose between the speakers—as still as an Egyptian statue, straining to hear. She got angry if I interrupted her enjoyment, and immediately demanded to be let out. I'm still wondering about the choice of that particular opera, and the blackness of that particular cat!

Gigi du Chah Name,
Black Persian, belonging to
Mrs. Elisabeth Kassis.

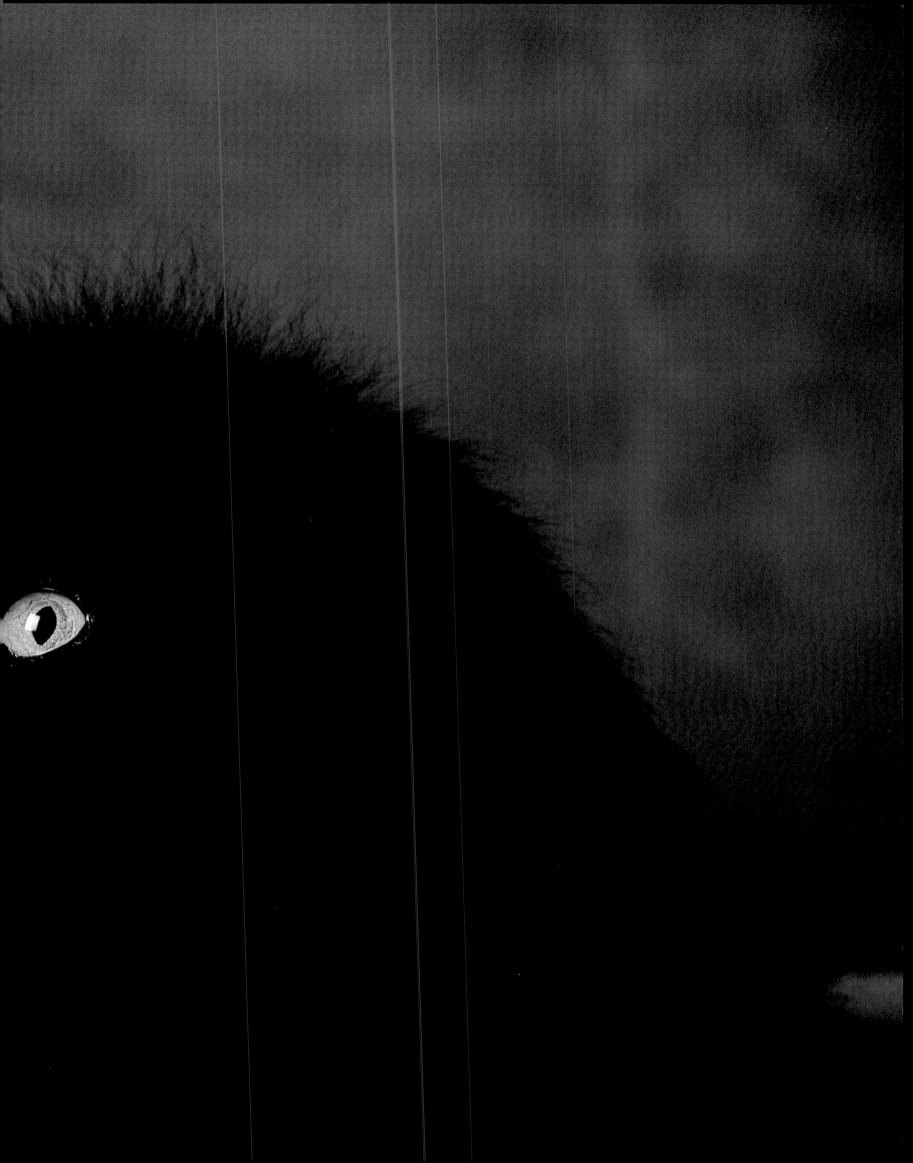

THE CAT AND THE PROPHET

We know that Mohammed, prophet of Islam, had great respect for his favorite cat Muezza. One day, she was asleep on the sleeve of his robe when he was called to prayer, and Mohammed decided to cut off his sleeve rather than wake the precious animal. Paradis de Moncrif recounts another anecdote concerning Mohammed: "Having the greatest esteem for Abdorraham, (he) wished to show this by giving him an illustrious name. The Arab custom was to be called 'father' of something related to one's behavior or one's talents;... of his many fine qualities, Mohammed was most inspired by Abdorraham's affection for a cat that he always carried in his arms, and chose for his companion the most honorable name of Abuhareira, 'father of the little cat'."

And Moncrif was not entirely wrong in adding: "At that time, Mohammed was just beginning his campaign of charm, and he weighed his every step; he was too political to call one of his disciples, to whom he wanted to give authority, the father of the cat, if the cat were not held in great esteem by the Arabs." Moncrif concludes: "In Mecca and Medina, it would no doubt have been a great disadvantage to be called father of pigs, since these animals had been proscribed by the Koran."

De Gazeau's Gicolin,
Tortie Smoke Persian,
belonging to Mrs. Brigitte Pottier.

TOM CAT

Léonor Fini claimed that the cat was female; certain languages seem to agree, and the animal has always been linked symbolically to woman... but, like it or not, it's sometimes a Tom! According to mythology, the Tom cat is the god, Atum, that protects the sun's barge on its nightly crossing; in legend, it's the devil at the witches' Sabbath. The mythical male cat, therefore, is a creature that has the power to do good... or evil. The modern feline that makes a name for itself in mass culture is decidedly masculine too: it's a figure of fun or irreverence, called Felix, Tom, Fritz, Sylvester or Garfield. The female cat is perfectly respectable... except when she's in love and is called Krazy Kat!

Elodée Magique des Lys Blancs, Silver Tortie Tabby Persian, belonging to Mr. Christian Maréchal and Mrs. Joëlle Riche.

CAT'S WHISKERS

The cat devotes a great deal of time to its furry little self; when it's not catching up on its beauty sleep, it can often be found at its ablutions. And when this extremely touchy, sensitive creature is disturbed, annoyed or caught off guard, it starts frantically cleaning a foreleg, as if something had dirtied it. Perhaps it feels sullied by some mysterious affront?

Fall River des Lys Blancs,
Black Silver Mackerel Tabby
Persian, belonging to
Mr. Christian Maréchal and
Mrs. Joëlle Riche.

PAWS FOR THOUGHT

"The cat was long held to be a diabolical creature. It had a thoughtful nature. It was supposed to be the witch's companion. Together with owls and horned beasts of strange shapes, it was part of the alchemist's usual material. The Middle Ages burnt witches, and sometimes scientists, so the cat had to burn with them. Great is the anger of brutes against thinkers."

CHAMPFLEURY

Daddy des Pujols of Royal Lys,
Blue Silver Classic Tabby Persian,
belonging to
Mrs. Marie-France Dendauw.

PARTNERS
IN WITCHCRAFT

On the subject of the cat's enemies in the Middle Ages, Champfleury tells us that according to the Scriptures (especially the Book of Revelations) the dog was the sorcerer's companion, whereas in the Middle Ages the cat was associated with the witch. He explains that the witch supplanted the sorcerer, as woman was considered familiar with the secrets of the heart, and therefore naturally capable of bewitching! So off she flies into the night sky, concocting evil spells, with her two typically feminine household attributes: the cat and the broomstick.

Doum-Doum du Pré du Curé,
Blue-Cream Persian,
belonging to
Mrs. Nicole Richefort-Tsango.

SACRIFICIAL VICTIM

The cat suffered great persecution and was the victim of ritual sacrifice from the Middle Ages until the nineteenth century. It was thought to symbolize evil, and was burnt for its devilry; in the Belgian city of Ypres it was thrown live from the top of the belfry on Ash Wednesday. After the winter at Carnival time, and in the summer solstice on Saint John's Feast day, cats were burnt alive on pyres throughout Europe to ensure plentiful harvests. A barrel full of cats was burnt every year at the Place de Grève in Paris, where the French monarch in person ignited the fires of Saint John. The future Louis XIII is said to have been horrified by this practice, and to have asked his father Henri IV to abandon it; it was finally abolished by Louis XIV.
In the countryside the cat symbolized grain, and was flailed to death on the threshing floor or buried between two furrows after the harvest. Apart from these sacrifices, which were linked to the agrarian cycle, there were also foundation rites which consisted of walling up live cats to impart their qualities—harmony of form and resistance—to new buildings; in the case of private houses, a cat buried under the threshold, sometimes with a rat, was supposed to protect the home against rodents. Mummified cats have been found in all kinds of buildings, including churches, proving that such practices were extremely widespread. As the Christian church was the enemy of witchcraft, it is surprising that it should have tolerated these rituals, which originated in ancient paganism, black Virgins and archaic fertility goddesses.

Grain de Sable des Embruns,
Cream Persian, belonging to
Mrs. Bernadette Haule.

"Hands reached out to hold me, rubbing me as if I were a soap against a belly or a cheek. But I was covered in fur... It did them good to rub me like that. It did me good too."

REMO FORLANI, *Gouttière*

CONFESSION

Unmasked! Here I am, the author of these pages, caught in the act of canoodling with a handsome Persian stranger. As far back as I can remember, I've always loved cats. All cats, from the well-groomed aristocrat sitting in state on its satin cushion, to the scruffiest of Toms showing off its scars on a street corner. As soon as I see a cat, I have to talk to it. I'm captivated by their air of unperturbable dignity, and invariably feel a desperate need to be recognized and accepted by such a superior species.

But I love them most of all for their fur. When I was little, I used to run and bury my face in a neighbor's mink coat (she found that very charming). So imagine the thrill of a real, live cat, a warm, clean-smelling, furry creature that stretches and purrs blissfully when it's stroked!

How wonderful to share my pleasure with the animal itself—the softest of coats and the biggest of teddy bears paled in comparison! The cat also shared my love of games—but its games were dangerous, because of its claws. To avoid getting hurt, I had to learn to be careful, to watch out for the slightest quiver beneath the fur, to become as cat-like as a cat itself, and to withdraw my fragile finger from its deadly paw just in time. If I let my attention wander or frustrated the cat once too often, the game turned nasty: the furious cat would lash out, or even bite... until we kissed and made up again.

What a miraculous creature it is, with its two-fold nature: a perfect little killing-machine, wrapped up in a soft and sensual exterior. My favorite fantasy would be to befriend a Siberian tiger... or better still, to be one! But, as reality tends to bring our dreams down to size, I'll just have to settle for loving cats!

Guizmo de Pomone,
Colorpoint Persian,
belonging to Mr. Jean-Yves Ramel.

"Jellicle Cats come out tonight
Jellicle Cats come one come all
The Jellicle Moon is shining
bright –
Jellicles come to the Jellicle Ball."
T.S. ELLIOT

THE IMAGINARY BALL

Mother Nature has dressed this black Persian for the ball, with its white ruff—no man-made mask could rival it at the Venice Carnival!
Let's imagine that strange voices have invited us to a ball; we take a seat in the gondola that sails along the misty canals to a phantom palazzo, half-way between a forgotten century and the castle

of the White Cat. There we find ourselves at the ritual Cats'Ball— we watch as the Moon Lake appears, during a secret ceremony conducted by the mysterious dogaressa Esclarimonda. The scene is from a story by Robert de Laroche: "In the shifting folds of the fabric on which Esclarimonda was standing, I witnessed the odyssey of cats throughout the ages... but of the many scenes which will always be engraved on my memory, I cherish above all the sight of groups of cats leaping and bounding through the night sky to meet the Moon. Cats drunk with freedom, leaping forward, then pausing for a moment on the rays of the night star, to

shake from their soft fur some specks of stardust which fall shimmering like silver...
What an indescribable feeling of peace came over me to behold the beauty of the Moon's black cats, gathered in meditation around pure-water springs, so far away in time and space, perfect, serene, untouchable, venerable and proud..."
But the dawn brings disillusion: near the church of San Zaccaria, the elderly Marietta feeds the very real local cats, then goes to pray at the feet of the Holy Virgin; as she bends down to kiss the ground, with feline grace and suppleness, the veil is torn aside: she is Esclarimonda, high priestess of a forgotten lunar cult.

Hursonne de Gremichka,
Black Smoke Persian,
belonging to Mrs. Jeanine Perdriol.

THE CAT HAS ITS REASONS

Perhaps T.S. Eliot best sums up the cat's contrariness, when he says of his Rum-Tum-Tugger:
 "For he will do
 As he do do
 And there's no doing anything about it!"
We all know the sort of cat that insists on fish when it's served chicken, that only enjoys the taste of cream when it can steal some, and will otherwise refuse it with disdainful paw; the cat that stubbornly refuses to explore the countryside all summer, and whose one desire, as soon as it's back in its apartment, is to escape. But if the contrary creature is always "on the wrong side of

every door," perhaps it has its reasons.
In his book *A Door into Summer*, science-fiction writer Robert Heinlein describes a cat called Petronius the Wise: "While still a kitten, all fluff and buzzes, Pete had worked out a simple philosophy. I was in charge of quarters, rations and weather; he was in charge of everything else... Regularly that winter, Peter would check his own door, refuse to go out of it because of that unpleasant white stuff beyond it (he was no fool), then badger me to open a people door. He had a fixed conviction that at least one of them must lead into summer

weather. Each time this meant that I had to go around with him to each of elevent doors, hold it open while he satisfied himself that it was winter out that way, too, then go on to the next door, while his criticisms of my mismanagement grew more bitter with each disappointment."
Inevitably, Pete the cat would end up going out, and "when he returned... he would glare at me and refuse to purr until he had chewed it all out... whereupon he would forgive me until the next time. But he never gave up his search for the Door into Summer."

*ABOVE: Foggy des Haudières,
Blue Persian, belonging to
Mrs. Catherine Fromal,
photographed with
Mr. and Mrs. André Jocquel.*

*RIGHT AND FOLLOWING DOUBLE
PAGE: Génaro de la Ronceraie
Desravine, Blue Persian,
belonging to Mr. Gérard Beroud.*

CATS
AND WRITERS

Colette's many cats inspired her writing, Cocteau was also a cat-lover and Baudelaire had a pathological obsession with the creatures. Other literary cat-fans include Emily Brontë, Lord Byron, Mark Twain, Raymond Chandler and Ernest Hemingway, among many others.

So what is it about the cat that appeals so much to writers and poets? Writing is mysterious work, a task that is accomplished in solitude and silence. The cat's very presence is a source of calm and quiet inspiration to the word-magician, who can travel through that profound, serene gaze like Alice through the looking-glass. The cat's physical presence—the silkiness of its fur, the warmth of its body—relaxes the tired mind, and the gentle vibration of its harmonious purr appeases the troubled soul.

Whether the cat is cleaning itself, playing its little games, or leaving paw-marks on the page, for the writer it represents a life without care: pure pleasure in the present moment, in the simple fact of existing—a pleasure that the author sacrifices in order to write. By looking into the cat's eyes, the writer reconciles him or herself to reality, and recovers a balance between the physical and the spiritual world.

Génaro de la Ronceraie Desravine.

THE CAT, THE CHILD AND THE KEY TO PARADISE

The cat features in a lovely legend, according to which the Heavenly Father was so angry with Adam and Eve for their misadventures with the snake and the forbidden fruit that he threw them out of paradise, with their sons and all their animals, and plunged the earth into total darkness. In the storm that followed, the path to heaven was lost to man and beast for ever. When day dawned at last, God remained deaf to human pleas and lamentations. No one grieved more desperately than Jacob, the third son of Adam. But the cat came to him and told him to dry his tears, for he, the cat who can see in the dark, had seen everything and could guide him back to paradise. Jacob took a strong walking stick and set off, with the cat for guide. They walked for a long, long time, crossing deserts and almost dying of hunger. Then one fine day, Jacob's stick burst into bud, and was soon covered in many-colored flowers: they had reached their destination and the gates of paradise were before their very eyes. The Angel of Light who guarded the gates had orders to let no mortal pass until the end of time. He was moved by their courage, however, and let them into the Heavenly dwelling, but for one hour only. He also allowed them both to eat a fruit, so that knowledge would be transmitted to them, and so that, on earth, there would always be a cat and a child who could find the path to paradise.

Trust of New World's Way
Good-Love, Silver Tortie Tabby
Exotic Shorthair, belonging to
Mr. and Mrs. Michel Sfez-Zon.

AN EXOTIC AMERICAN

With its curious figure and moon-like face, the Exotic Shorthair looks like a total stranger but is in fact a short-haired Persian. It first appeared in the U.S., initially as a "variant" in two separate breeding programs; one was intended to strengthen the quality of the American Shorthair with Persian blood, and the other wanted to introduce the color Chocolate into the Persian breed by crossings with Burmese. The Exotic Shorthair breed was fixed in the 1960s; its conformation is the same as that of the Persian, so it has the same Standard.

PRECEDING DOUBLE PAGE AND RIGHT: Phalaenopsis Emile Victor, Red Tabby Exotic Shorthair, belonging to Ms. Christelle Ponthieu and Mrs. Claudine Naels.

ABOVE: Tasha Isatis of Follow Me, Blue Point Exotic Shorthair, and Hilary Tom Pouce Follow Me, Cream Point Exotic Shorthair, belonging to Mr. Régis Machin.

SECRET IDENTITY

What are you thinking about behind your frown and your closed eyelids, red cat? What kind of rogue are you, with your proud mustache? You make me think of a Scottish fisherman, sitting at the back of a dark pub, surrounded by leather and polished oak, lost in thought with his pipe in his mouth and a pint of beer in front of him. Or maybe you're a Cheshire cat, preparing to vanish and leave nothing but your grin—and your whiskers—behind you!

SCIENTIFIC OBJECTIVITY

"The cat is an unfaithful domestic that we keep only from the necessity of setting him at another, even more incommodious domestic enemy that we are unable to hunt... Although these animals, especially when young, have a certain sweetness, they also possess an innate malice, a perfidy of character, a natural perversity, that all increase with age and that education merely masks. When education has done its best, from determined thieves they become fickle, flattering scoundrels: they have the same skill, the same cunning, the same taste for evil, the same penchant for petty theft; they too know how to cover their tracks, dissimulate their designs, apprehend opportunities, bide their time, choose the moment to make their move, then elude chastisement, flee and keep their distance until summoned to return. They acquire with ease

society's ways, but never society's morals; they have only the appearance of attachment. This can be seen in their oblique movements, in their equivocal eyes; they never look the loved one in the face; from distrust or duplicity, their approach is devious, and the caresses they seek are for their selfish pleasure."

BUFFON, *Natural History* (1758)

LEFT: *Tasha Isatis of Follow Me*
RIGHT: *Hilary Tom Pouce of Follow Me*

"One thing was certain, that the white cat had had nothing to do with it: it was the black kitten's fault entirely."

LEWIS CARROLL,
Through the Looking-Glass

CAT'S GOLD

It used to be thought that certain cats, preferably black ones, had magic powers which enabled them to find gold for their masters. Consequently, they were well fed, and sometimes even wore little purses around their necks so that they could set off at nightfall to "do their duty." Many a poor cat lost its life on account of this belief, when it proved incapable of bringing home the smallest gold coin to its gullible owner... and some unscrupulous people were condemned by the courts for selling these "gold cats" at exorbitant prices.

Many stories and legends illustrate the notion of the "cat with the golden touch," including Charles Perrault's *Puss in Boots* with its false "Marquis of Carabus," and the story of Dick Whittington, the poor boy who became Lord Mayor of London once his cat had made his fortune by ridding a foreign kingdom of its rats.

These stories and many others originate in the same tradition, which was probably universal, as there are Buddhist and Sufi variations on the same theme. The "cat's gold," which was wrongly interpreted by vulgar minds, in fact represented the wealth of knowledge. In all these tales, the poor or unhappy hero finds happiness after passing the various tests that require him to trust his cat. The cat guides the hero to wisdom, and his new-found material wealth symbolizes his transformation. The cat's alchemic gold, of knowledge and transmutation, takes us back to Egypt and to Bastet, who watched over the successive rebirths of Osiris. For we must not take the cat at face value, but go with it through the looking-glass, beyond surface appearances.

Gitane de Nid d'Amour,
Blue Silver Tabby Exotic Shorthair,
belonging to
Mr. and Mrs. Michel Sfez-Zon.

CATS

This chubby-cheeked character with its teddy-bear face is the final representative of our aristocratic cats; perhaps we should let the fictional Esclarimonda, Venetian dogaressa and High Priestess of cats, conclude in its honor: "Look at them closely, when you advance toward them... What do you see? That cats are never ugly, nor vulgar, nor low, nor depraved. Their inner beauty always shines through. Even in their old age they are Beauty incarnate, and there is grace in their every movement..."

Cake Bread Drambuie,
Blue Mackerel Tabby Exotic
Shorthair, belonging to
Mr. and Mrs. Michel Sfez-Zon,
photographed with
Mr. Alain de Lavalande.

A LAST LOOK

What fascination there is in the cat's eyes, in that unblinking stare that draws and disturbs us, in those pupils that can narrow to a vertical slit or widen beyond measure to devour the colored iris.

We feel an aesthetic satisfaction when we admire a cat, but to look into its eyes is an unsettling, even frightening experience. Even the most enthusiastic of cat-lovers feels a vague fear, mingled with respect. No doubt this disturbing sensation is due to some feline devilry… if the eyes are the windows of the soul, the cat's eyes hold no comfort or reassurance for us, and its unflinching, undecipherable stare is devoid of all affection. And yet that unreadable eye is not empty—it seems to have access to an opaque and mysterious presence beyond. To look deep into the cat's eyes is to be aware of its absolute "otherness," and it requires great peace of mind to endure such a trial with equanimity.

When we look into the cat's eyes, we penetrate to the very heart of its "mystery"—if mystery it is. The puss that we scold for sharpening its claws on the sofa immediately assumes a suitably guilty expression, but there is not the slightest hint of remorse in its eyes. And when it abandons itself to our caress, we receive no loving looks in exchange—its whole body expresses its pleasure, but there is no change of expression in its half-closed eyes. It stretches out a furry paw, and spreads its toes in delight, demonstrating its feelings by gestures… the literal meaning of the word "emotion," after all, is "outward movement." Whether it is hunting or killing its prey,

"And specks of gold,

like fine sand,

are sprinkled like distant stars

in their mystical eyes"

CHARLES BAUDELAIRE

lying in the sun or waiting for the magical fridge door to open at dinner-time, looking at a plate with thoughts of theft or grooming itself, the cat observes the world around it with its objective, unwavering eye. Only the angle of its head, ears and whiskers, and the tension in its neck, back and tail betray the intensity of its concentration and its readiness to make a move. To understand a cat, one must learn its body language: like a perfect Zen soul, its eye is a non-reflecting mirror.

So is the cat Zen? According to a Buddhist legend, at the death of Buddha all the animals gathered, but only two remained dry-eyed: the cat and the snake. Along came a mouse, which began to lick the oil from a funeral lamp. The cat immediately pounced on it and gobbled it up. Consequently, two schools of thought grew up regarding the creature: either it was an infamous, heartless beast that added insult to injury by committing murder, or else it was a wise animal, able to see through the illusory veil of sentiment and to react as the laws of nature dictate.

This legend once more demonstrates the cat's duality: angel if we love it and admire it for its "otherness"; devil if we hate it and find it disturbing. As for the cat itself, it still goes by its "wild lone," ears pricked and tail held high, while man theorizes to his heart's content and my own pussycat sleeps, curled up against the purring computer, pink nose on white paw, secure in the knowledge that she is The Cat, leaving us humans to ponder all the other questions.

INDEX

Cats are no longer burned, and the ones thrown from the belfry at Ypres are now toys... but they are still abandoned by people who assume they will survive, and leave them to their fate: the lucky ones—sick, terrified, down to skin and bones but alive—are taken in by animal shelters.

Cats at the "Logis du Boncé" animal shelter, photographed with Mme Thérèse Arnac

BIBLIOGRAPHY

WORKS CITED IN THIS BOOK:

BAKER, Stephen, *How to Live With a Neurotic Cat,*
Random House, 1999.

BAUDELAIRE, Charles. *Les Fleurs du mal,*
Gallimard, "Poésie" series, no. 85, 1972.

CARROLL Lewis, *Alice's Adventures in Wonderland
& Through the Looking Glass,* Watermill Press, 1992

CHAMPFLEURY. *Les Chats,* Éditions Les Silènes, 1992.

CHATEAUBRIAND, René de, quoted by Robert Delort.
Les animaux ont une histoire, Seuil, "Points Histoire" series,
no. 174, 1993.

COLETTE. *La Paix chez les bêtes* and *Autres Bêtes,*
Gallimard, "La Pléiade" series, complete works, volume II.

DE SIMONE, Roberto. *La Gatta Cenerentola,*
Éditions Einaudi, Turin, 1981.

ELIOT, T.S. *Old Possum's Book of Practical Cats,*
Harcourt Brace & Co., 1982.

FINI, Leonor. Preface to *Histoires et légendes du chat,*
Tchou, 1992.

FORLANI, Remo. *Gouttière,* Gallimard,
"Folio" series, no. 2282, 1991.

HEINLEIN, Robert A. *Door into Summer,* Random House,
1998.

KIPLING, Rudyard. *Just So Stories,*
William Morrow & Company, 1996.

LAROCHE, Robert de. *Chat noir miroir des songes,*
Éditions Judith Henry, 1986.

LOTI, Pierre. *Vies de deux chattes,* followed by *Chiens et
chats,* Éditions Alain Quella-Villégier, Pardès, 1988.

MONCRIF, Paradis de. *Histoire des chats,*
Éditions Robert de Laroche, Pardès, 1988.

PEIRESC, Nicolas Claude Fabri de, letter quoted by
Laurence Bobis in *Les neuf vies du chat,* Gallimard, "La
Découverte" series, no. 105, 1991.

VALÉRY, Paul. "Tiger," in *Mélange,* Gallimard,
"La Pléiade" series, complete works, volume I.

FURTHER READING

AMORY, Cleveland. *Cleveland Amory's Compleat Cat,*
Black Dog & Levanthal, 1995

BECKER, Suzy. *All I Needed to Know I Learned from My
Cat,* Workman Publishing, 1998.

BESSANT, Claire; *Cutts,* Paddy; and *Viner,* Bradley.
Cats: The Complete Guide, Barnes & Noble Books, 1999

COLETTE. *La Chatte,* Gallimard,
"La Pléiade" series, complete works, volume III.

FORLANI, Remo. *Ma chatte mon amour,* Ramsay, 1992.
Tous les chats ne sont pas en peluche, Gallimard,
"Folio" series, no. 2158. 1990.

JOYCE, James, *The Cat and the Devil,* Moonlight
Publishing, 1988 (out of print).

LAROCHE, Robert de. *Le chat dans la tradition spirituelle,*
Éditions Judith Henry, 1984.
     Chats de Vénise, Casterman, 1991.
     Histoire secrète du chat, Casterman, 1993.

LÉAUTAUD, Paul. *Bestiaire,* Grasset,
"Les Cahiers rouges" series, no. 126, 1990.

NEYE, Emily. *All About Cats and Kittens,*
Putnam Publishing Group, 1999.

Original title: CHATS
Written by: Danielle Laruelle
Adviser: Sabine Paquin, International Feline Judge
Photographs by: Yann Arthus-Bertrand
Art Direction: Philippe Pierrelée,
assisted by Sophie Domenach
Layout: Anne-Marie Le Fur
Editor: Marie Renault, assisted by Laurence Basset
Published by les Editions du Chêne - Hachette Livre 1993
© 1993, Société nouvelle des Editions du Chêne

English editor: Lisa Davidson
Translator: Sally Laruelle
Copyright © 2000 Editions du Chêne - Hachette Livre.
All rights reserved.
This edition published by Barnes & Noble, Inc.,
by arrangement with les Editions du Chêne.
© 2000 Barnes & Noble Books
M10987654321
ISBN : 0.7607.2217.X